Methuen Playscripts

The Methuen Playscripts series exists
to extend the range of plays in print by
publishing work which is not yet widely
known but which has already earned a
place in the repertoire of the modern
theatre.

Plays for Public Places

This volume contains three plays, each of which
illustrates a different approach to the task of writing
a play for a specific occasion. Gum & Goo, a 30-
minute play about a disturbed child, was first performed at an educational conference. Wesley lasts 60
minutes, the normal length of a Methodist service, it
was performed in a Methodist church at the 1970
Bradford Festival. John Wesley's life is acted out in
a series of episodes, to which the singing of Charles
Wesley's hymns acts as a commentary. Scott of the
Antarctic, a savagely ironic attack on the cult of
heroism, was performed on an ice rink at the 1971
Bradford Festival. The three plays illustrate the range
of one of the most promising of the new British playwrights. They also reflect the growing interest of many
playwrights, directors and actors all over the world
in taking drama into many different public places and
bringing it to audiences who never go to the theatre.

By the same author

Revenge
Christie in Love and other plays

PLAYS FOR PUBLIC PLACES

Gum & Goo

Wesley

Scott of the Antarctic

HOWARD BRENTON

First published in Great Britain 1972
by Eyre Methuen & Co Ltd
11 New Fetter Lane, London EC4P 4EE
Copyright © 1972 by Howard Brenton
SBN 413 28740 8 HB
SBN 413 28750 5 PB

Printed in Great Britain by
Redwood Press Limited, Trowbridge, Wiltshire

To Chris Parr

Contents

Author's Note

Gum & Goo was written at the Brighton Combination in January of 1969. A Teachers Conference asked for a show. There were eight days to make something. We kicked ideas around for two days from a scene I'd written about a little girl down a hole. I wrote the script in the next two days. The remaining four days we rehearsed it.

The play was formed by thinking of whom it was being done for (the teachers), where (a gymnasium floor with two big lights and a possible blackout), and who was free to do it (two big blokes, James Carter and myself, and a girl, Katya Benjamin). Ruth Marks directed us.

So the play was 'tailor-made'. A response to an invitation to perform, with what was to hand - three actors, a few days, a budget of thirty shillings for a ball and three bicycle lamps.

Wesley was commissioned and directed by Chris Parr for the 1970 Bradford Festival.

It was written to be performed in Eastbrook Hall, Bradford, a Methodist church. The church seats a thousand. There is a gallery all round, in which the choir sit. The organ is central, above the choir. The pulpit is a preaching pulpit, the concentrated point of the building's sight lines. The 'playing space' referred to in the script is a long, narrow strip of floor between the communion rail and the front pew, right across the width of the church, raised by rostra.

The elements of the show are the John Wesley actor (Bruce Myles in the Festival production), the company of actors, and the choir.

The show depends on these elements being kept strictly to their functions. (For example, actors do not go into or sing with the choir.)

The John Wesley actor develops his performance in great detail and rhetorical display.

The company of actors frame his performance. While the John Wesley part is ambiguous, the other parts are meant to be immediately obvious.

The choir should be as large as possible, and above all LOUD. The hymns are sung fast. Charles Wesley set his hymns to pop tunes of the day. The choir is in uniform dress, but only for the visual effect of a human backdrop. (They don't wear surplices.)

The play is a giant blow-up of Wesley's account of his faith. 'LADIES AND GENTLEMEN. WE GIVE YOU JOHN WESLEY. THE DARK NIGHT OF HIS SOUL. HIS STRUGGLE WITH SIN WITHIN. HIS STRUGGLE TO KNOW GOD. HIS JOURNEY TO SALVATION. '

Scott of the Antarctic (or What God Didn't See) was commissioned and directed by Chris Parr for the Bradford Festival of 1971.

The text published here is a scenario as well as a play text. A number of people collaborated on the show, bringing their vision to it.

The actors were from the University of Bradford Drama Group. The skaters were from local clubs. I set their music, Vaughan Williams's Sinfonia Antarctica, but left them to arrange what passages they thought suitable for the spots. I asked for them to be all in white, including faces, hands and legs.

Jeff Nuttall designed the costumes, Mary Restieaux made them. Huge, gangling, gaudy apparitions - like adverts stepped down from the billboards of some rubbish world (adverts for God, Jesus etc.).

John Dowling made the tape.

The pop songs were written and performed by the New Portable House Band.

Roland Miller designed the lighting.

Roland also performed in the show. At its conception, we had a long discussion of aims. We then worked strictly apart. He had the idea of working with the show, but in no way as part of it.

At the performance, as the audience went in Roland sat on the pavement outside, a shivering figure, his explorer's costume torn to the flesh and pitifully inadequate for the Bradford night, let alone the Antarctic. On the rink he slunk through the action, always on the edge of the spots. He clutched a teddy bear (he was interested in Scott's complex attitudes to the animals with the expedition). He haunted the show, a kind of anti-Scott, carrying all the wretchedness and personal suffering.
H. B.

GUM & GOO

Gum & Goo was first performed by the Brighton Combination in January 1969, with Katya Benjamin, James Carter and Howard Brenton. Directed by Ruth Marks.

Performed many times throughout 1969 and 1970 by the Bradford University Theatre Group, with Michele Ryan, Greg Philo and Phil Emmanuel. Directed by Chris Parr.

(Their performance of this piece was very fine: I've used their names for the parts in the script.)

Performed by the Royal Shakespeare Company at the Open Space at lunchtime in February 1971. Directed by Janet Henfrey.

As the audience come in, GREG, PHIL and MICHELE are playing touch-he, in a circle.
The audience sit all around.
When they're all in, the game goes on for a while.
A plastic football's thrown into the circle.
They pick it up, throw and bounce it about, off the walls, on the ceiling, it's fun.
It stops being fun. The two boys begin to hog the ball.
Piggy in the middle starts. It's fair at first.
But MICHELE gets stuck in the middle.
GREG and PHIL torment her, hide the ball behind their backs, hold it above her head; she goes on tiptoe to try and get it.
Suddenly, GREG throws the ball to MICHELE.
Delighted, she throws the ball to PHIL, to start the piggy game again.
But the boys play dead, let the ball roll away.
She tries again to get them to play, but they just stand still.
She gives up, sad. Sits down, lets the ball roll away.
Stands up, turns away, sucks her thumb.

GREG: There's that goofy kid again. Goofy!

PHIL: Goofy goofy!

GREG: Goofy goofy!

(GREG goes up to her.
Pause.
Then suddenly he lifts her skirt with his toe.)

GREG: She's got corrugated knickers on, 'cos she wets her-
self!

PHIL: Goofy goofy!

GREG: Goofy goofy!

(A pause.)

GREG: 'Ere. I bet her Dad's a gorilla.

PHIL: I bet her Ma's a Ford Cortina.

GREG: Don't be stupid. A gorilla and a Ford Cortina can't
have sex.

PHIL: Yeh, they can.

GREG: Can't.

PHIL: Can.

GREG: Can't.

PHIL: Can.

GREG: Where would the gorilla put it in then? That's what I'd
like to know. Where would he put it in?

PHIL: In her petrol pump!

GREG: Up her exhaust!

PHIL: Smash right through her rear window!

GREG: You've got a dirty mind for a twelve-year-old.

PHIL: Yours in't bad, and you're eleven.

(A pause.
They stare at MICHELE.)

GREG: Eh, goof. Tell us what your Ma's like.

(A pause.
Then MICHELE goes down on her knees and mimes an igloo
shape.
The boys are nonplussed.)

GREG: Looks like an igloo.

> (MICHELE mimes a door.)

> It is an igloo. That was the door.

> (MICHELE crawls through the 'door' and snuggles up.)

> What do you make of that?

PHIL: Freak in her head, in't she? My Dad says they all should be put away, all them communists and freaks. My Dad says put them away.

GREG: 'Ere. You ever thought what it's like to be a nut?

PHIL: If I were a nut?

GREG: If you were a nut, what would you do?

PHIL: I'd do. . .

> (Thinks. Then he gets excited.)

> Women in! With a knife!

> (PHIL mimes raising a knife and stabbing.
> He lurches about, attempting a horror face and walk.)

GREG: What you doing?

PHIL: I'm doing women in with a knife, 'cos I'm DOCTOR CRIPPEN.

> (He stabs away.)

GREG: You don't look like Doctor Crippen to me.

PHIL: I'm going to Doctor Crippen you in your gut.

> (PHIL makes a lunge at GREG. They fight, roll over on the floor, kicking and struggling. Then they roll apart, tired of the game.)

> You know what Doctor Crippen did? When he'd done 'em in, he put 'em in a bath, nude. And all the blood SPURTED out in the water. Then he bottled the bathwater and drank it on Sundays.

GREG: That weren't Crippen.

PHIL: That were!

GREG: It weren't! It were Haigh.

PHIL: It were Crippen and I read it in a book called Crime does not Pay.

GREG: Anyway, Crippen, Haigh, they were nothing to Adolf Hitler.

(MICHELE moans quietly.)

PHIL: My Dad says, Hitler was a man terribly wronged.

GREG: My Dad says Hitler was the biggest bad man who ever lived. And Winston Churchill got him: BANG.

(MICHELE's moaning grows.)

Winston Churchill stood on the cliffs of Dover in his battle-dress and he made this speech 'bout filling up the hole with the English dead. Then Winston Churchill took out this great big gun and he SMASHED Adolf Hitler.

(MICHELE's moaning becomes a scream.)

PHIL: Eh. Look at her.

(MICHELE begins to rock backward and forward, moaning. The boys are panicky.)

GREG: She's goofy.

(They shout at her.)

PHIL: Oy! Iron knickers!

GREG: Goofy!

(MICHELE's screams and rocking become horrible, then suddenly stop.
She's dead still, eyes closed.
A pause.)

I think she's dead. You think she's dead? She's dead.

PHIL: Na, she's fainsy. Oy kid!

(Nothing from MICHELE.)

GREG: She's dead.

(GREG and PHIL stare at each other.
Blackout.
In the blackout, at once. GREG speaks the following dead-pan, that is as fact and not poetry. PHIL whispers the words almost simultaneously, but not quite - a fraction after.)

The dark inside.
The light inside the dark inside.

The beautiful lands inside.
The lovely ladies in the fields inside.
The silver children and the animals at play inside.
The snows, and Christmas-is-forever inside.

(MICHELE, at once, with a cutting, official doctorish voice.)

MICHELE: In the extreme condition, the child's senses are totally dislocated. Fire is cold, cold burns. Words screech. Animate objects are stone. The child walks on another planet, converses with beings not conceived of by the natural world.

(And at once, GREG and PHIL switch hand lamps on. NB: At the Brighton Combination, we had these set on the floor. That was a bit ugly, we had to find them in the blackout. In the production by the Bradford Theatre Group and the RSC they carried the lamps in their pockets. GREG and PHIL as Gum & Goo. Grins. They overlap their cues to each other, their words tumble over each other.)

GREG: Mary.

PHIL: Mary.

GREG: Mary Mary Mary.

PHIL: Mary had-a-little-lamb Mary.

(Lamps onto MICHELE, who stares straight ahead.)

MICHELE: Who you?

GREG: I Gum Gum.

PHIL: I Goo Goo.

GREG: He Goo Goo.

PHIL: He Gum Gum.

(Lamps on MICHELE.)

MICHELE: What you?

(Lamps on GREG and PHIL.)

GREG: We Gremlins, Mary.

(Lamps on MICHELE.)

MICHELE: Grem-lins.

(Lamps on GREG and PHIL.)

GREG: He Gremlin Goo, I Gremlin Gum.

(GREG and PHIL nod frantically, then lamps on MICHELE.)

MICHELE: You good, or you bad?

(Lamps back on GREG and PHIL.)

GREG: We good Mary. In't we Goo?

PHIL: Yeh, we good. Very very good.

GREG: We very very very good.

(GREG and PHIL nod frantically.)

Not bad.

(GREG and PHIL shake their heads.)

PHIL: We not bad.

GREG: We not ever bad. 'Cos we're good.

(GREG and PHIL nod.)

We your friends Mary.

PHIL: Yeh, we your friends.

GREG: You want us be your friends?

(Lamps on MICHELE.)

MICHELE: You. . . my. . . friends?

(Lamps on GREG and PHIL.)

GREG: We your friends. You don't need other friends, when you got Gum and Goo.

PHIL: Gum and Goo, friends with you.

GREG: Gum and Goo do what you want to do, Mary. Mary, what you want to do?

(Lamps onto MICHELE.)

MICHELE: Where the lovely ladies are and. Go there. It's Christmas. And where the animals are. And where it's magic all day and. And.

(A pause.
The lamps stay on MICHELE.)

GREG: You go there Mary.

PHIL: You go there.

MICHELE: Go now?

GREG: Not now Mary.

PHIL: Not now Mary.

GREG: You go home now Mary.

MICHELE: I want to play.

GREG: We play. But not now.

PHIL: Go home Mary.

GREG: Go home and have your tea. And don't tell.

PHIL: Don't tell.

GREG: Don't tell, on Gum and Goo.

(Lamps out.)

MICHELE: Gum. Goo.

(Lights up. GREG and PHIL are standing.
MICHELE stands up.)

Sometimes I go funny, and I fall down. And.

(A pause.)

But then I stand up. An' I go home for tea.

(A street scene.
GREG as a business man, hailing a taxi.
PHIL as a policeman, directing traffic.
Then as men in the street, walking about turning corners.
This technique is a straight crib from the Freehold's
'Street Scene'.)

GREG: Taxi!

(A pause. GREG watches a taxi passing him, hails one
coming the other way.)

Taxi!

(GREG and PHIL move toward each other, in a square
figure.
They recognize each other, smile, shake hands.
They at once move on, blank faced,
Walk to other corner of the square, where PHIL bumps
GREG on the shoulder and walks straight on.

GREG turns on him in an ugly way.
Then PHIL stops still.
GREG walks up and down, 'waiting for a bus', looking at
his watch.)

MICHELE: The streets in our town are funny an' I get lost.
An' I get scared.

(Goes up to PHIL.)

'Scuse me mister, can you tell me where a toilet is?

(PHIL moves on, then freezes.
MICHELE goes up to GREG.)

'Scuse me mister, can you tell me where a toilet is?

(GREG ignores her, still waiting, then freezes.)

An' when I'm scared I think. I think I'll burn the whole
world down. That's what I think. I'll burn the houses down
and burn the mums and dads down. I'll burn my mum and
dad down. Specially my mum. I'd like to see my mum's
hair burn and hear her scream. She screamed once when
I threw the iron at her. It made a funny mark on her face.
I'd like to see her silly legs up burning and her knickers
turning black. And when all the world was burnt I'd. I'd.
BE HAPPY.

(PHIL, as the mother, mimes taking an apron down, tying
it round her waist, smoothing her hair. Comes into the
centre, and starts kitchen work.
GREG as the father, in another room, reading a news-
paper.
The mother's soppy.)

MICHELE: Mummy Mummy.

PHIL: Not now Mary.

(A pause.
MICHELE sulks, calculating.)

MICHELE: YOUR HAIR'S ON FIRE.

PHIL: WHAT?

(She clutches her hair. Then arranges it, tired, back to
work.)

Oh Mary, you're telling lies again.

MICHELE: It was.

(A pause.
MICHELE sulks, calculating.)

MICHELE: LOOK, A RAT.

PHIL: AHH. WHERE?

MICHELE: UNDER THE COOKER.

PHIL: AHH.

(A pause.
Mother on her toes.
She calms down.)

Oh Mary, that was another lie, I don't know what makes
you tell them. You mustn't tell lies.

(She goes back to work.)

MICHELE: What's for tea?

PHIL: It's bread and butter, and that nice raspberry jam
you like. I got some in specially.

MICHELE: I bet it's rat. I bet it's rat for tea. Rat on toast.

PHIL: Mary, what a wicked thing to say to your mother.

MICHELE: Rat rat rat! You give me rat for tea, you ratbag.

PHIL: Mary!

(MICHELE jumping up and down.)

MICHELE: Ratbag ratbag ratbag.

(PHIL slaps MICHELE's face.
MICHELE stops jumping,
stares,
then howls.
PHIL at once mortified.
MICHELE puts all the agony on, falls down on the floor,
howling.
PHIL leans over, trying to get her to stand up.)

PHIL: Don't cry, Mary, I'll get you ice-cream for tea.
Mary, don't cry. Pink and green ice-cream, you like
that. Don't cry Mary. Strawberry ripple ice-cream
Mary...

(MICHELE grabs her mother's hair.)

Mary Mary Mary let go my hair!

(GREG comes in as the father.)

GREG: Mary! Let go your mother's hair at once!

(MICHELE does so, and turns on her father.)

MICHELE: Daddy rat, the biggest rat of all.

(She hits her father in the balls.)

GREG: OOOOH.

(He doubles up.)

MICHELE: I'm going out to play, and I hope you BURN.

(MICHELE turns away.
PHIL as mother, clutching hair.
GREG as father, clutching crotch.)

PHIL: What did we do to deserve such a child?

GREG: Don't distress yourself, my love. We must have
patience.

PHIL: Patience.

GREG: Patience.

PHIL: But what did we do, and where did she get those
thoughts?

(They freeze in their contorted positions, as MICHELE
does her speech.)

MICHELE: I was playing with my mum, and I got hold of her
head, and it roll off. Under the table. And I run down the
garden. And my mum's head it roll after me. And I go in
the shed. And I shut the shed and. My Mum's head it
bump against the door bump bump bump. And say let me
in Mary, Mary let me in.

(MICHELE draws the igloo, and goes into it.
PHIL crouches down at the side of the playing area, out of
it for the moment.
GREG goes into an old man, going round the circle working
in a limp, a drag of the limping leg, swinging of an arm,
cough, spit and stoop. Stops by MICHELE.)

GREG: Oy Miss. You got a penny on you?

MICHELE: Why? You want to go to the toilet?

GREG: Maybe I do, and maybe I don't.

(GREG's old man gets a bag of sweets out of his coat, mimed.)

MICHELE: You a dirty old man? You got some sweeties?

GREG: Have a sweetie.

MICHELE: You are a dirty old man. You'll be my very own dirty old man.

(MICHELE goes to take a sweet, but GREG suddenly withdraws the bag.)

GREG: I was in the war. I made the dead. You alive, or dead?

MICHELE: ImmmmmmmmmmDEAD.

GREG: Wa?

MICHELE: I'm a ghost. Waaa Waaa.

(GREG turns away.)

Oy Mister, don't go away. Tell me 'bout the dead.

GREG: Wa?

MICHELE: I saw a film about the dead. It were Dracula. I got into see it through the exit door. It were <u>Dracula Has Risen from the Grave</u>. There were lots of blood.

(GREG jerks and begins to turn round.)

Dracula got stuck on this cross right through his heart. That were good. An' he bit a lovely lady in the neck. That were very good.

(Change.)

But half-way through the film I went funny.

GREG: The dead lie with rotting eyes. And the Lord calls, and they rise up. Have a sweetie.

(MICHELE takes one.
GREG, at once.)

I got a place.

MICHELE: What, a secret place?

GREG: Out there.

(GREG gestures.)

MICHELE: Out on the rocks? It's creepy there.

GREG: There.

MICHELE: It your Dracula tomb?

 (MICHELE stands.)

 Let's go there mister, go there and play.

GREG: Wa?

 (GREG takes her by the hand. They go along together.
 MICHELE saying 'We play biting lovely ladies' necks
 an' crosses through your heart. . . ' etc.
 PHIL stands. As policeman. Walks towards them.)

PHIL: Hello hello hello.

MICHELE: Look out, it's a copper.

PHIL: Sweeties, is it?

GREG: Wa?

 (PHIL grabs GREG's arm, twists it. GREG's old man
 goes down.)

PHIL: Child fingerer are you? Child fingerer, eh? Scum
 you are. Scum on the milk of society.

MICHELE: Let him go, copper.

PHIL: Finger kids eh, finger kids eh?

GREG: Ahh!

MICHELE: Let him go, let him go.

PHIL: It's all right, my love, you're safe now.

MICHELE: Let him go, he's my dirty old man not yours.
 You fucking copper.

 (MICHELE pummels the policeman's back.)

PHIL: 'Ere! You little cow. I'll deal with you later.

MICHELE: He's mine. We was going to play Dracula then
 you came, you fucking copper. My dirty old man and me,
 we were gonna bite the lovely ladies in the neck. And it
 would snow, and then you come along you FUCKING
 COPPER.

 (MICHELE stamps her foot, and turns away.)

PHIL: She's run off, and I've not got her name and address.

But I still got you. You're a catch, sonny boy. We've not had a child fingerer down the station for weeks. It'll be drinks all round on the Inspector tonight!

(PHIL and GREG freeze, as the copper twisting the arm of the old man.)

MICHELE: All go away. Way way way. All go. Dirty old man, don't go.

(Blackout.
Gum & Goo again.)

GREG: Mary.

PHIL: Mary.

(Lamps on GREG and PHIL.)

GREG: Gum not go.

PHIL: Goo not go.

GREG: We stay and play with you.

(Lamps on MICHELE.)

MICHELE: Play now. You play now.

(MICHELE stamps her foot.
Lamps on GREG and PHIL.)

GREG: Not here.

PHIL: Not here Mary.

GREG: Out there.

PHIL: Out there.

GREG: Out the rocks Mary.

PHIL: We play out there.

(Lamps on MICHELE.)

MICHELE: But I not got my old man. And there big boys out the rocks. It scary. There... Holes out there. I not go out the rocks if I not got my old man.

(The lamps remain on her.)

GREG: But you got Gum.

PHIL: You got Goo.

GREG: We with you alway.

PHIL: Gum and Goo alway with you.

    (They're suddenly nasty to her.)

GREG: Go there!

PHIL: Go there!

    (Sweetly.)

GREG: Mary.

PHIL: Mary.

GREG: See ya.

    (Lamps out.)

MICHELE: See ya Gum. See ya Goo.

    (At once lights up, GREG and PHIL as the boys, straight into it...)

PHIL: I been reading this book 'bout Al Capone. 'Bout how he had this bullet proof limousine. And 'bout how he slayed hundreds. Hnnnnnnnnnnnnn.

GREG: Al Capone was nothing.

PHIL: Al Capone was not nothing. He was the biggest slob America has known and he slayed hundreds.

GREG: He was useless.

PHIL: He was tough.

GREG: He was a useless criminal.

    (A pause.)

    And anyway, Superman smashed him.

PHIL: Superman!

GREG: Superman smashed Al Capone with his super powers.

PHIL: You don't believe in Superman.

GREG: What if I do?

PHIL: Superman's for kids.

GREG: We're kids.

PHIL: But Superman. I bet you believe in Batman too.

GREG: Well?

PHIL: How stupid. How

    (Mispronounces.)

    unutterably stupid. My Dad says them mags are

    (Mispronounces.)

    unutterably stupid.

GREG: I seen you reading them.

PHIL: Where?

GREG: In the bog at school.

PHIL: That weren't Superman. That were Doctor Death.
    Doctor Death would crush Superman any day.

GREG: Wouldn't.

PHIL: Would.

GREG: Wouldn't.

PHIL: Would. Anyway, if Superman did crush Dr Death the
    RED SKULL would have revenge, 'cos of his invincibly evil
    brain.

GREG: Rubber man would crush the Red Skull anyday.

PHIL: Rubber Man? He's just a wet bit of elastic.

GREG: He's not! He's the Great Stretcho. He can knock a bad
    man out half a mile away 'cos his arm's like a rubber
    band. It shoots out with his mighty fist at the end of it,
    POW.

PHIL: POW.

GREG: POW.

PHIL: POW.

GREG: Then Captain America would sweep in with his mighty
    shield of freedom and ZAP all in sight. ZAP!

PHIL: ZAP!

GREG: ZAP!

PHIL: ZAP!

GREG: Be great to be a super hero.

PHIL: Be great to be a super villain.

GREG: It's getting dark.

PHIL: Yeh.

(A slight pause.)

GREG: Super villains get powed and zapped all the time.

PHIL: I'd not be. Soon as Superman and that lot came on the scene, I'd be off. Probably to Majorca with the great train robbers.

GREG: You couldn't escape the forces of good.

PHIL: Na?

GREG: Na.

PHIL: Bet I could.

GREG: It's really dark.

(A pause.)

PHIL: Not going, are you?

GREG: I just said it's dark.

PHIL: You scared?

GREG: You know what they say 'bout the rocks?

PHIL: What, ghosties?

(PHIL snorts.
MICHELE comes forward.)

GREG: It's the freak. Maybe the freaks come up here at night.

PHIL: What, and have it off with the ghosties?

(To MICHELE.)

Hello freak. What you doing up here? Little kids should not come up here in the darkies.

MICHELE: Play.

PHIL: What?

MICHELE: Want to. Play.

GREG: Freakie, freakie...

PHIL: Cut it out.

(To MICHELE.)

You want to play? What you want to play? I'm not going to hurt you kid. What you want to play?

(MICHELE, suddenly.)

MICHELE: I wanna play TOMBS. An' DEAD MEN. An'
BITING NECKS. An' KICKING MY MUM'S HEAD.

(Innocently.)

You play with me?

(PHIL, nonplussed.)

PHIL: Yeh. Well. What do you reckon?

GREG: Yeh. Well. Could have a game or two.

MICHELE: I wanna play rotting eyes an' the dead rising up.

(A pause.)

GREG: Let's push off.

PHIL: No we're going to play. With the kid. We'll play with
you kid, but the kind of games little kids should play. Like
cowboys and Indians. Right? There's one thing though, kid.
You're the Indian, right? And we're the cowboys, right?
Bang. Bang.

(GREG stands awkwardly by.)

Come on!

(Together they go bang bang and pistol firing noises near
MICHELE.
But there's nothing from her, she just stands there.)

Oy kid. Indians –

(Hand to his mouth.)

Go oyoyoyoyoyoyoyoyoyoyoyoyoyoyoy. Go oyoyoyoyoyoyoy.

(MICHELE makes the movement to her mouth, but silently.)

GREG: Let's push off.

(PHIL is incensed at her.)

PHIL: Oyoyoyoyoyoyoyoyoyoyoyoyoy.

(PHIL gets GREG to join in. They do an Indian dance round
her, then bang bang as cowboys. PHIL grabs her from
behind.)

PHIL: We got you Indian! We got you Indian! We got the dirty
little Indian savage!

GREG: Yeh we got the Indian!

PHIL: Dirty Indian savage, you're our prisoner now!

(A pause. Both breathless, excited.)

Let's put our prisoner down that hole.

GREG: What?

PHIL: She's our prisoner! Put her down that hole!

(PHIL drags her aside roughly, shoves her down the hole, shouts down at her.
Do this by having MICHELE 'down the hole' to one side, looking up, and GREG and PHIL looking down at the floor to one side of her.)

You go down that hole you dirty dirty Indian.

(He's hysterical, near tears.)

And don't talk about the dead.

(A pause.
Then GREG, tentatively.)

GREG: She in't saying anything.

(A pause.)

You oughtn't to have put her down there.

PHIL: It was only a game.

(A pause.)

Kid. Game's over.

(They look at each other.)

GREG: You oughtn't to have.

PHIL: Kid.

GREG: Kid.

PHIL: Kid.

GREG: Kid.

PHIL: Kid.

(A pause.)

I got to go home now.

(A pause.)

Oy, kid. You all right down that hole?

(GREG and PHIL look at each other, then turn and run.
Blackout as they're running.
A SECTION OF EFFECTS:
In the blackout, in their own words for a few sentences
each, GREG, MICHELE and PHIL each tell what they
thought Heaven was like when they were kids.
A pause.
Then MICHELE switches on a handlamp, moves it round the
ceiling, begins a wail.
GREG and PHIL come in, switching lights on, playing
them round the ceiling, the 'wailing' has a canon effect.
Experiment showed that using a common sound, 'M', then
each taking a word, Mary/Margarine/Miranda, and
sliding over the vowel sounds in your word, made the
desired effect.
This builds up. When MICHELE goes into a scream, cut it.
And snap the lamps out.
A pause.
Then MICHELE switches her lamp on, shining it up into
her own face. She looks up.
GREG, as the father, switches his light on the ground,
going all over the place.
PHIL, as the Police Inspector, shines his on the ground
too, but his search is methodical.)

GREG: She ran out of the house.

PHIL: Oh yes sir.

GREG: Ran out.

(A pause. They're looking on the ground...)

Mary! Mary!

PHIL: That won't do much good sir. Why don't you go and have
a nice cup of tea.

GREG: You will find her.

PHIL: Oh we'll find her.

GREG: Inspector, over here!

(A pause.)

No. Inspector, over here!

(A pause.)

No.

PHIL: Let us handle it sir. We're used to it. Kids go down, in and up anything. We handle it.

(A pause.)

GREG: Mary's a difficult girl.

PHIL: They can be difficult.

GREG: Wilful.

PHIL: They can be wilful.

GREG: Not bad.

PHIL: No, not necessarily bad sir.

GREG: She has thoughts.

PHIL: They do have thoughts sir. You try and stop kids having thoughts, but they go right on and have them.

GREG: I don't know where they come from.

PHIL: That would be 'The age we live in', sir. Constable! Give those dogs fresh scent. You were saying, sir?

GREG: I was saying. What was I saying?

PHIL: I see them all. All the bad bits. The indecencies. We had one up here not long ago, an indecency.

GREG: Why don't you fill this place in?

PHIL: Ancient monument sir. Preservation Order.

GREG: But it's dangerous!

PHIL: Still ancient. Still a monument.

GREG: Mary! Mary!

PHIL: All right sir. Here she is.

(Their lamps together on one spot,
MICHELE continuing to look up.
She's not dead – worse, she's silent.)

GREG: Mary.

PHIL: Mary.

GREG: Mary.

PHIL: Mary.

GREG: Mary.

PHIL: Mary.

GREG: Mary.

> (GREG and PHIL put their lamps out. MICHELE still
> looking up for a few seconds, then she puts her lamp out.
> End play.)

WESLEY

Wesley was first performed at the 1970 Bradford Festival on February 27 by members of the Bradford University Drama Group, directed by Chris Parr.

Characters

JOHN WESLEY
MR WESLEY
MRS WESLEY
FIRST VILLAGER
SECOND VILLAGER
CHARLES WESLEY
FIRST UNDERGRADUATE
SECOND UNDERGRADUATE
THIRD UNDERGRADUATE
FIRST SAILOR
SECOND SAILOR
THIRD SAILOR

FOURTH SAILOR
FIFTH SAILOR
MORAVIAN MAN
MORAVIAN WOMAN, with a baby
MORAVIAN BOY
AMERICAN COLONIAL FARMER
FIRST AMERICAN COLONIAL WOMAN
SECOND AMERICAN COLONIAL WOMAN
AN AMERICAN INDIAN
FIRST DEVIL
SECOND DEVIL
ANNOUNCER

CHOIR: the combined Methodist and school choirs of the district.

SCENE ONE

The CHOIR are seated in their places.
When all of the audience are in, the actor who speaks the announcements comes forward.

ANNOUNCER: LADIES AND GENTLEMEN. JOHN WESLEY, FOUNDER OF METHODISM, PREACHES TO YOU.

(The CHOIR stand.
The JOHN WESLEY actor comes on, unhurriedly, and mounts the pulpit.
A pause.)

JOHN: Man did disobey God. He ate of that tree. And in that day, was he condemned. The sentence whereof he was warned began. For the moment he tasted that fruit, he died. His soul died. Likewise his body became corruptible. Dead in spirit, dead to God, dead in sin he hastened down to death. Down, to fire.

(With a gesture he accuses the audience.)

Thou! Ungodly! Thou vile, helpless, miserable sinners! Go, ungodly, guilty, lost, destroyed, dropping into Hell! And being so debased, undone, helpless, and damned sinners, look unto Jesus!

(The CHOIR speaks the reply.)

CHOIR: LOOK UNTO JESUS.

JOHN: Look unto Jesus! The lover of thy soul! Torn and bleeding he was, for thee! Look unto Jesus!

(The CHOIR speak the reply.)

CHOIR: LOOK UNTO JESUS.

JOHN: Plead thou no good works. No righteousness. No humility. No contrition. No sincerity. Plead thou only the blood. Blood of the Lamb of the Covenant. The ransom paid by God crucified. The blood! Paid for thy proud and sinful soul.

(JOHN turns aside, overcome.
The CHOIR sing.
JOHN leaves the pulpit and stands to one side.)

CHOIR: Jesu, lover of my soul,
Let me to thy bosom fly,
While the nearer waters roll
While the Tempest still is high.
Hide me, O my Saviour, hide
Til the storm of life be past.
Safe into the haven guide
O receive my soul at last.

(The CHOIR remain standing.
An announcement.)

ANNOUNCER: LADIES AND GENTLEMEN. WE GIVE YOU JOHN WESLEY.

(He indicates the WESLEY actor.)

THE DARK NIGHT OF HIS SOUL. HIS STRUGGLE WITH SIN WITHIN. HIS STRUGGLE TO KNOW GOD. HIS JOURNEY TO SALVATION.

(A pause,
while the CHOIR sit.)

SCENE TWO

The actors of JOHN's parents take their place.

JOHN: I was born in the year seventeen hundred and three. In the Parish of Epworth. The son of Samuel Wesley, Rector of that Parish. He was a man of God. But my mother was the stronger.

MRS WESLEY: Samuel!

MR WESLEY: Yes, dear heart?

MRS WESLEY: Break the child's will.

MR WESLEY: Yes, dear heart.

MRS WESLEY: Break the child's will, for God.

MR WESLEY: Yes, dear heart.

MRS WESLEY: You hear, children? Be broken for God.

(Women's voices in the CHOIR and JOHN answer 'Yes Mamma'.)

And never think like your father.

(Women's voices in the CHOIR and JOHN answer 'No Mamma'.)

Fear the rod, and cry softly.

(Women's voices in the CHOIR and JOHN answer 'Yes Mamma'.)

Samuel?

(A pause.)

MR WESLEY: Yes, dear heart.

MRS WESLEY: I cannot pray for the King of England.

(MR WESLEY angry and about to reply. But he turns away.)

You hear me? I will not do what you would have me do.

MR WESLEY: No, dear heart?

MRS WESLEY: Pray for that usurper, William of Orange.

(MR WESLEY loses his temper.
He throws his hat on the floor.
He looks at his wife.
He jumps up and down on his hat.
He points at his wife.)

MR WESLEY: Jacobite!

MRS WESLEY: Whig!

MR WESLEY: Popery's dupe!

MRS WESLEY: Parliament's fool!

MR WESLEY: William is King!

MRS WESLEY: James!

(MR WESLEY jumps up and down on his hat again.
Then controls himself.
A pause.)

MR WESLEY: Woman. If we are to have two Kings, we must
have two beds.

MRS WESLEY: On your conscience be that.

(MR WESLEY is furious, but he subsides.
Gently.)

MR WESLEY: Sukey...

MRS WESLEY: Conscience. The voice of God. We must heed
conscience, and break the will. It is hard, Samuel. But the
way of God is hard.

MR WESLEY: Yes, dear heart. Yes, dear heart.

(Head bowed MR WESLEY turns away and makes his way
slowly up to the pulpit during the next speech.)

JOHN: And my father weaker than her but proud, turned to
his true love, the Book of Job.
My father hated England. The sodden landscape. The dull
and violent peasantry.
His spirit groaned. Weighed down by English mud.
His heart was in Sinai. The desert, with Moses.
Not the filth of an English rural slum.
By night high in the house, rain on the window mist over the
roof my father saw in his mind's eye the pillar of fire. He
saw the prophets. In a country of fire.
Angels rose up in the heat.

Chariots came from the sun.
My father was an English Job.
Job in an old English house with rising damp.
Job stranded in the Lincolnshire fens.
Broken by his wife.

(MR WESLEY has reached the pulpit, and opened its Bible.
He turns the pages at random, pointing at random to
various passages.
All are from the Book of Job.)

MR WESLEY: Let the day perish wherein I was born
And the night which said 'There is a man child conceived.'
Let the day be darkness!

(He turns the page, reads again.)

For the arrows of the Almighty are within me.
The poison whereof my spirit drinketh up.

(He turns the page, reads again.)

My Soul is weary of my life.
I will give free course to my complaint
I will speak to the bitterness of my soul.

(He turns the page.
He bends over the Bible, following the words silently with
his finger.
Below on the playing space, two VILLAGERS pass.
They look up at the pulpit.
It's to be taken as MR WESLEY's study window in this
passage.)

FIRST VILLAGER: Parson Wesley.

SECOND VILLAGER: Ay. Parson Wesley.

(FIRST spits.
SECOND spits.
A pause.)

SECOND: Studying late o' night.

FIRST: Ay. Bloody books.

SECOND: Ay. Bloody books.

FIRST: Popery in books.

SECOND: Ay.

FIRST: Devil's work! That's what be in books.

SECOND: That's what be in books, all right.

(At once the FIRST VILLAGER comes forward with his speech to the audience.)

FIRST: Parson's in 'is Rectory House, reading books. There be two kinds o' Parson. Your bookish and your 'unting. Your bookish parson, 'e's all for clever sermoning and fancy Greek. Your 'unting parosn, 'e's all for scaring poor cows to death with 'is view hallo and bloody roar.

SECOND: 'Is bloody roar!

FIRST: And what of us, eh? The agricultural workers, poor sods. I'll tell you. Our gut rots! All the day long, in mud. God-less. Penni-less. And the land's no more than a bog, lump of mud. And lump of mud the man who works it. 'Is kiddies and 'is wife, all soaked. On the rot. And your parson, 'e closes 'is carriage door. Spouts Greek. 'E blows 'is bleeding 'unting 'orn.

SECOND: 'Is bleeding 'unting 'orn!

FIRST: And not being a reader o' Greek, or a reader o' 'owt, come to that, and not being an 'unting man 'cos I's not got the cash for an 'unting 'orse or any of the fancy tackle and being what's more a LUMP OF MUD...

(He turns and shouts up at the MR WESLEY actor.)

The agricultural worker, a dead loss. Eh Parson? No Greek. No 'unting 'orse. And no soul either, a dead loss! Eh Parson?

(The MR WESLEY actor ignores that, and reads on.)

In't I right Billy?

SECOND: You are Ted.

FIRST: What we do Billy?

SECOND: Dunno.

(Pause.
Then they continue, indicating they're drunk from this point.)

FIRST: Go round 'is cows? Maim 'em?

SECOND: Break their knees.

FIRST: Wring 'is chicken.

SECOND: Fire 'is ricks.

FIRST: Burn 'is house down.

> (At once
> the CHOIR stand,
> the VILLAGERS turn to the audience and make the
> announcement.)

SECOND: LADIES AND GENTLEMEN. EPWORTH RECTORY
GETS BURNED DOWN.

FIRST: JOHN WESLEY IS SEVEN YEARS OLD.

SECOND: JOHN WESLEY IS SAVED FROM THE FIRE.

> (The VILLAGERS turn to the pulpit, and shout up at the
> MR WESLEY actor.)

> Parson Wesley!

FIRST: Parson Wesley!

SECOND: What about us, then!

FIRST: What about us, then!

> (The VILLAGERS, joined by others of the cast throw brands
> into the pulpit.
> These can be bundles of red paper, with streamers
> attached.
> The MR WESLEY actor is at first oblivious to the shower
> of fire, and reads on. But then he looks up in horror, arms
> out wide.)

MR WESLEY: Fire! Fire! A fire not blown by man shall
devour him!

JOHN: The house blazed. In the horrid confusion, the child
was left asleep in the attic. He woke to fire all about. Hell
fire sucked to breathe him in. The baby was in the jaws!
He climbed to the window. Against flame, he showed himself to those below. And God plucked him forth. I am that
baby. I was lost, destroyed, dropping into hell! I was a
brand. Plucked out of the burning. For God.

> (The CHOIR sing.)

CHOIR: Where shall my wondering soul begin,
How shall I all to heaven aspire,
A slave redeemed from death and sin,
A brand plucked from eternal fire,
How shall I equal triumphs raise
Or sing my great Deliverer's praise?

(A pause, while the CHOIR sit.)

SCENE THREE

At Oxford.
No announcement for this scene.
THREE UNDERGRADUATES of the University of Oxford lounge
about at one side. One has a cricket bat, one a hoop and stick,
one a cup and ball.
The JOHN WESLEY actor comes onto the playing space.
Then the CHARLES WESLEY actor comes forward.

JOHN: Charles. Welcome to Oxford.

(CHARLES turns round about, sees John, and smiles.)

CHARLES: Jack!

(They embrace.)

FIRST UNDERGRADUATE: 'Pon my soul 'nuther Wesley bwuvver
come up. Wot?

SECOND: Wot?

THIRD: Wot?

SECOND: Damme. A buruvver? Two of em? Wot?

FIRST: Wot?

THIRD: Wot? An is 'e 'oly too?

FIRST: Damn 'oly. Too 'oly. Two of 'em, too 'oly. Wot?

(He gives a nasty little laugh, as if he's made a joke.)

Ha!

SECOND: Ha!

THIRD: Ha! Wot?

FIRST: Wot?

SECOND: Wot?

CHARLES: Who are these fellows Jack?

JOHN: Undergraduates of the University of Oxford.

CHARLES: Those pigs?

JOHN: They are of the age, Charlie. Pray with me.

(CHARLES is taken aback.)

CHARLES: What here? In the quad? And in full view?

JOHN: Pray with me. I want you to.

CHARLES: Of course, Jack.

(JOHN and CHARLES kneel down to pray.
The SECOND UNDERGRADUATE stands, incensed at the sight.)

SECOND: Damme and blast me eyes. They're akneeling down.

FIRST: Akneeling down?

SECOND: Akneeling down, apraying!

THIRD: Akneeling down apraying? Wot, in the air?

FIRST: Akneeling down apraying? An' not in church?

SECOND: Gad. They've gone too far.

FIRST: Somewhat excessive.

SECOND: Excessive? Apraying in the air excessive? I'll tell you what apraying in the open air is!

(He goes purple with anger.
A pause.)

FIRST: Well?

SECOND: Atheism!

(A pause.)

And Popery!

(A pause.)

Wot?

FIRST: Wot?

THIRD: Wot?

(They're all steamed up.
But their bubble of anger bursts, and they sink back into lounging about.
JOHN and CHARLES stand.
Then the SECOND UNDERGRADUATE starts off again, disgruntled.)

SECOND: Damn unhealthy thing, religion. Encourages rickets,

on account of being kneeled down all day.

THIRD: But them Wesleys do take exercise. Tennis.

(And the SECOND UNDERGRADUATE is incensed again.)

SECOND: Tennis? Tennis? There's a damned unhealthy thing. Give me a round of rummy. Cards! Now there's exercise.

(JOHN speaks to the audience, like an announcement.)

JOHN: The body is God's gift. It is beholden to us to give it good strength.

(JOHN and CHARLES mime a tennis match, with actual rackets, but with net and balls mimed.
John serves.)

JOHN: Pat.

CHARLES: Pit.

JOHN: Pat.

CHARLES: Pit.

JOHN: Pat.

CHARLES: Pit.

(JOHN hits harder.)

JOHN: Pat!

(CHARLES fails to return.)

CHARLES: You have me!

(CHARLES mimes picking the ball up, and tossing it back to JOHN.
He 'catches' the ball and serves.)

JOHN: Pat.

CHARLES: Pit.

JOHN: Pat.

CHARLES: Pit.

JOHN: Pat.

CHARLES: Pit.

JOHN: Pat.

CHARLES: Pit.

JOHN: Pat.

CHARLES: Pit.

   (JOHN hits harder.)

JOHN: Pat!

   (CHARLES is beaten by the shot, but this time doesn't pick
   up the ball.)

CHARLES: John. You have a hangdog look.

   (A pause.)

JOHN: Play tennis.

   (CHARLES frowns,
   then shrugs.
   Picks the ball up.)

CHARLES: The pigs say you're too religious.

   (JOHN says nothing.)

   The stupid pigs say you're touched.
   The clever pigs say...

   (But changes his mind.)

   No matter.

   (He throws the ball to JOHN.
   JOHN catches it.)

JOHN: What do they say? The clever pigs.

CHARLES: No matter.

JOHN: Charlie! What?

CHARLES: The sin of Intellectual Pride.

   (John stares at him.
   A pause.)

JOHN: Play!

   (JOHN serves.)

   Pat.

CHARLES: Pit.

JOHN: Pat.

CHARLES: Pit.

(But JOHN suddenly makes no attempt to return.)

JOHN: That may be one of my sins. I am convinced of my sins, Charlie.

CHARLES: What sins?

JOHN: Many. Many, foul thoughts. Damning me, Charlie.

CHARLES: Rubbish. Rubbish. Utter cant.

(JOHN attempts to reply, but goes and gets the ball.)

Look in the World. There sin is lodged. With the poor, like beasts. The criminal. The wretch like a demon gone to murder. The rich man, lascivious. There godlessness lives, which I take to be the name of sin. Vile. The Devil's work.

(He scoffs.)

But not so in you, John Wesley. Parson from a country backwater. Scholar of Oxford.

JOHN: In me.

CHARLES: Rubbish. Rubbish. Utter cant. Play tennis.

(JOHN serves,
while speaking.)

JOHN: But my sins cry out.

(CHARLES returns the ball.
JOHN returns the ball.)

Boasting!

(CHARLES returns the ball.
JOHN returns the ball.)

Greed. Greed of praise.

(CHARLES returns the ball.
JOHN returns the ball.)

Intemperate sleep.

(CHARLES returns the ball.
JOHN returns the ball.)

Heat in argument.

(CHARLES returns the ball.
JOHN returns the ball.)

CHARLES: You fool. You've got no sins.

(With that line, CHARLES returns the ball very hard and beats JOHN all ends up.)

JOHN: We are all fallen.

CHARLES: You no more than most.

(JOHN picks up the ball and serves.)

JOHN: Pat.

CHARLES: Pit.

JOHN: Pat.

CHARLES: Pit.

(JOHN returns, hard.)

JOHN: Pat!

(CHARLES tries to reach the ball for a return, but stumbles.)

It is not light matter! Charlie, for what was I saved from the fire? To damn myself? To cover myself in mine own filth? To weigh me down, by mine own hand to weigh me down? To go back again to Hell mouth, truly deserving of eternal pain? For that?

(CHARLES shouts.)

CHARLES: I don't know.

(A pause.)

JOHN: I tell you. For this reason was I saved from the fire.

(JOHN turns to the audience.)

That I, John, by mine own hand, should work Mine Own Salvation.

<u>SCENE FOUR</u>

JOHN helps CHARLES up.
Note: they've got to get rid of the rackets.
They walk, in conference with each other.

JOHN: Charlie. I am to preach to the University.

(CHARLES stops.)

CHARLES: To the pigs?

JOHN: My text will be: 'Which of you convinceth me of sin? And if I say the truth, why do ye not believe me?'

CHARLES: Just the stuff for pigs.

(CHARLES makes a snorting noise.
JOHN walks slowly up to the pulpit.
CHARLES takes a seat in the front pew.)

FIRST UNDERGRADUATE: Here's a fine hallyballo. The Wesley fellow, e's marked down to preach.

THIRD: Wot? To th' University?

SECOND: Preach? That...

(He goes purple.
A pause.)

Satanist?

FIRST: And to th' University.

SECOND: By thunder. He shall not!

FIRST: E's marked down.

SECOND: I'll protest! To the Bishop! To the Archbishop! To th'Almighty 'Imself!

FIRST: E's marked down.

SECOND: Lads, I think we go to church.

THIRD: To church? Wot us?

SECOND: And have a wheeze.

(He nudges his friends.)

Wot?

FIRST: Ah. There's an excellent thing.

(The THREE UNDERGRADUATES sit in the front pew.
An announcement.)

ANNOUNCER: JOHN WESLEY PREACHES AT ST MARY'S, OXFORD,
TO THE UNIVERSITY.
HE ANGERS THE CONGREGATION.
FOR THE FIRST TIME HE IS BANNED FROM A PULPIT.

(The JOHN WESLEY actor, in the pulpit, stands.

(The CHOIR stand with him.
They sing.)

CHOIR: Come, oh my guilty brethren, come,
Groaning beneath your load of sin.
His bleeding heart shall make you room,
His open side shall take you in.
He calls you now, invites you home,
Come, oh my guilty brethren, come!

(The CHOIR sit.)

JOHN: From the eighth chapter of the Gospel According to St.
John, the forty-sixth verse. 'Which of you convinceth me
of sin? And if I say the truth, why do ye not believe me?'

(The rowdy UNDERGRADUATES erupt.)

FIRST: 'E takes the text from the Book of John! Book of 'is
own name!

THIRD: Thinks 'e's the Evangelist hisself. Come back down
among us, to tell us all what's what.

SECOND: There's mischief in it! Do not heed the text!

(He turns round in his seat and shouts at the audience.)

Do not heed the text!

(JOHN begins the sermon.)

JOHN: At what age. . .

(But the SECOND UNDERGRADUATE shouts again to the
audience.)

SECOND: All damn mischief! Heed none of it!

(JOHN begins again, very loudly.)

JOHN: AT WHAT AGE, DO WE FEAR GOD?

(The SECOND UNDERGRADUATE whirls round, glares up
at JOHN.
JOHN stares back at him.
The UNDERGRADUATE subsides.)

SECOND: Huh.

(A pause, then JOHN begins again.)

JOHN: At what age, do we fear God?

(A pause, then quickly.)

When I first came into this world, I saw my mother. My
father. The kindly house. I grew. I came to know the fields,
the marsh flat for miles. The look of ordinary England,
the ordinary clouds. All was drab. Comforting. Real. It
was my home.

(Then grandly, pointing up then down.)

But at what age did I know that over the ordinary landscape
RISES THE MIGHTY VAULT OF HEAVEN, THAT BELOW
BOIL THE PITS OF HELL?

(A pause, then quietly.)

At what age did I know, that Man crawls on a fallen world.
Suspended by a single thread from heaven, I mean the Grace
of Christ, above that terrible abyss. That man is a
creature of filth. A lover of the dark. At what age did I
know...

(His hand to his chest.)

I sin.

(JOHN holds the gesture while the UNDERGRADUATES
speak.)

THIRD: 'E do speak prettily. 'E do come on rather about sin,
but he do speak prettily.

SECOND: If y'ask me, 'e do speak ripely. Over-ripely.

JOHN: My friends, I do not know when the awesomeness of
creation, that terror of Heaven and Hell, came to me. That
I was, even as a child, a soul damned, corrupted by Adam.
Oh yes, I gnaw at such profundities. I argue with relish.
Oh yes, I tug at theology with the best of you, a dog with
a bone, and not let go. But know? What do I know? Only
this, I know. That I stand here. Damned. A convinced
sinner.

(He becomes sarcastic.)

Ha! Who is not persuaded to think favourably of himself?
'Tis now quite unfashionable to say anything to the dis-
paragement of human nature, which is generally allowed
to be very innocent. Very wise, very virtuous. There are
writers most universally read, admired, applauded, who
hold man to be very innocent, very wise, very virtuous.

(He becomes adamant.)

But I tell you. I tell you the scripture. 'In Adam all died'. That fallen, sinful Adam 'begat a son in his own likeness'. Therefore we are 'dead in sins, without hope, without God in the world'. 'The Children of Wrath'. 'I was shapen in wickedness, and in sin did my mother conceive me. '

FIRST: 'Pon my word.

SECOND: I say.

FIRST: 'E speaks against 'is own Mamma!

THIRD: But 'e quotes from scripture, direct. 'E's clever.

SECOND: Clever y'call it, do you, clever! It's a disgrace, and ought not to be allowed!

JOHN: I tell you the Scripture. 'The Lord looked down from Heaven upon the children of men. He saw they were all gone out of the way; they were altogether become abominable, there was none righteous, no, not one. ' Not I.

(He points about the audience.)

Not you. Not you. Not you. Not you.

(He points at the SECOND UNDERGRADUATE.)

Not you.

(The SECOND UNDERGRADUATE is on his feet at once, and forward, at the foot of the pulpit.)

SECOND: Sir!

(A silence.)

Sir! You speak of English Gentlemen.

JOHN: Sir, I speak of all men.

(The SECOND UNDERGRADUATE fumes.)

SECOND: Do you speak of English Gentlemen, sir?

JOHN: Of all men, sir.

SECOND: Don't shilly-shally with me, sir! Do you speak of English Gentlemen?

JOHN: I speak of all men. English. All.

SECOND: And what do you say of English Gentlemen, sir?

JOHN: I say all are sinners.

SECOND: Withdraw that remark, sir!

JOHN: No, sir.

SECOND: And why not, sir?

JOHN: Because it is true, sir.

> (The UNDERGRADUATE fumes.
> JOHN is dead still.
> Suddenly the SECOND UNDERGRADUATE turns and eyes the audience.)

SECOND: And what of the King?

> (A pause.)

JOHN: The King, sir?

SECOND: The King.

> (CHARLES stands, but at a loss.
> He looks from the UNDERGRADUATE up to JOHN.)

The King, sir. The greatest English Gent of all.

> (He turns on JOHN.)

D'you call His Majesty Sinner? At front of all this loyal congregation, d'you call the Royal Personage 'Filth'? A Sinner?

> (He points at JOHN.)

Answer, sir!

> (A parenthesis device here: the SECOND UNDERGRADUATE points at where JOHN is.
> JOHN stares at him, opens his mouth.
> But then whirls away and stumbles half down the pulpit steps.
> The SECOND UNDERGRADUATE holds the gesture at the pulpit while JOHN speaks to CHARLES.)

JOHN: Charlie. I must speak Truth. And what truth?

CHARLES: The Word of God.

JOHN: And what Word is that? Logos Word of God, 'I am the Word'. And what word? Dog? That the Word? Dog? That the Word to say? Stand before all the congregation, say DOG?

> (To the audience, wildly.)

Dog, I say to you. Dog. Dog. Kneel! To y'prayers! Tremble in y'boots sinners! Live in fear, scum on the waters under heaven! Y'days are numbered! For I say DOG.

CHARLES: Shut up.

(Pause.)

Shut up John.

JOHN: Charlie. Remember that night.

(He whispers.)

We saw the Devil.

CHARLES: We had fasted too much. We saw things not there...

(JOHN cuts across him.)

JOHN: We were kneeled down. At prayer. Five hours we were kneeled down. In silence. And prayed, from the marrow of our bones, with every ounce of flesh, beseeching God. Together, in the bare room, in the dark, hour after hour. Then just before dawn, we began to laugh.

CHARLES: The lack of food. We were tired.

JOHN: We were wide awake, and laughing! Like girls all agiggle. Unholy and profane, oh, the joker got to us. And when the fit had passed we lay exhausted. And slunk off. We could not look each other in the eye. Or speak... of Old Nick! On his haunch in the corner! Cracking 'em to us!

CHARLES: John!

JOHN: Charlie! What if the joke's still on, eh? What if now, I, in church, speaking over the Book itself, look... Up here!

(He rushes back up into the pulpit, puts his hand on the Bible.)

What if I stand here? At centre of church. Doing the Devil's turn? Eh, Charlie, what then?

CHARLES: Shut up, man.

(CHARLES points to the UNDERGRADUATE.)

Shut up man. Don't faff about. Speak to him, a simple word.

(The SECOND UNDERGRADUATE breaks from pointing at the pulpit.)

SECOND: Answer, damn you sir.

(A pause.)

JOHN: Sir.

(A longer pause.)

Sir, let us each look to himself. We must seek salvation.
For the love of God, I advise you to do so. As for myself...

(He speaks to all the congregation.)

I would be mine own self's surgeon. On God's altar take
the knife. Cut out mine own soul. Hold it in my hands. A
bloody cankered thing. Cut out that nauseous part, the
human part, I mean my sin. That I may be cured.

(A gesture all around.)

All you, do likewise. For the love of God I do advise it.

(The SECOND UNDERGRADUATE turns to the audience,
and during the following speech storms out of the church,
up an aisle and out a back door.)

SECOND: 'E does not answer. 'E insults the Body Royal! I
tell you, this fellow, he'll run amock. All over. 'Is damned
theology, s'all devilry! And sedition! We'll be up to our
necks in 'is mess 'fore long, mark me. The whole of
England, loaded up with 'is damned nonsense! Personal
salvation eh? That 'is game eh? Bull. Bull the lot of it.
And dangerous. Drive poor people out their 'eads. Then
wot? Arson! Destruction of property, and persons. He's
an uppity parson and uppity parsons we do not want. No
sir. Burnt 'em a hundred years ago. Burn 'em today I
say. Atheists, Pope-lovers, witches and trouble-makers.
Burn 'em all.

(He's at the back. He turns and speaks to all.)

Mark you this, one man so obsessed, so taken over, will
take others over. He'll have the whole of England off their
'eads! Wailing on about sin. Burn 'im. Burn 'im now.

(He goes out of the church, slamming the door.
JOHN is shaken, a pause.
Then quickly.)

JOHN: In the Name of the Father the Son and the Holy Ghost

amen.

(The CHOIR stand.
JOHN goes from the pulpit fast down to CHARLES.)

SCENE FIVE

JOHN and CHARLES are on the playing space at the front of
the church.
CHARLES makes up a hymn, and as he makes it up the CHOIR
sing it - that's the idea of this scene.

JOHN: No. Simple. Word.

CHARLES: You chew on things, Jack. Sing a hymn with me.

JOHN: I have no voice. No words. No. . .

(With a gesture of dismissal, turning around.)

Principle within.

(CHARLES muttering.
JOHN is groping for a monologue about himself, CHARLES
is picking up the phrases and making them into a hymn.)

CHARLES: Principle within. Principle within.

JOHN: No. . . godly fear.

CHARLES: I want a principle within
Of Jealous godly fear.

That's it!

I want a principle within
Of jealous godly fear.

(Organ sounds the note.
The CHOIR sing.)

CHOIR: I want a principle within
Of jealous godly fear.

(CHARLES skips back and forth excitedly.)

CHARLES: What rhymes? Within. Sin of course. Fear. What
can we have with fear. Near? Near will do. But so will
appear. What appear? Angels appear. Seraphim, they
appear.

(But he's doubtful, strokes his chin.)

JOHN: I need a sensibility, of sin. A pain to feel.

CHARLES: A sensibility of sin
  A pain to feel it near!

  (Delighted, he claps.
  The organ sounds the note.
  CHOIR sing.)

CHOIR: A sensibility of sin
  A pain to feel it near.

  (A short pause, then the CHOIR sings the whole verse.)

  I want a principle within
  Of jealous godly fear,
  A sensibility of sin,
  A pain to feel it near.

JOHN: It's all pride with me! Our mother was right. Watch
  the will, its heat.

  (CHARLES spells out the next lines.)

CHARLES: I want the first approach to feel,
  Of pride or fond desire,
  To catch the wandering of my will
  And... Douse

  Not douse. Douse is not good.

  (At once, lighting up.)

  Quench!

  (Quickly.)

  I want the first approach to feel,
  Of pride or fond desire,
  To catch the wandering of my will
  And quench the kindling fire!

  (The organ sounds the note and the CHOIR sing.)

CHOIR: I want the first approach to feel,
  Of pride or fond desire,
  To catch the wandering of my will
  And quench the kindling fire!

  (CHARLES at once,
  straight off.)

CHARLES: That I from thee no more may part,

No more they goodness grieve
The filial awe, the...

(He's stuck.)

Tum... Ti... Tum. Tum... Ti... Tum.
The tum... Ti... Tum.

(JOHN suddenly gives him the phrase, harshly.)

JOHN: The fleshly heart.

(CHARLES stares at him.)

CHARLES: The fleshly heart.

(A slight pause.)

The tender conscience give.

(They make up the rest of the hymn together.)

JOHN: Quick as the apple of an eye
O God my conscience make.
Awake my soul, when sin is nigh
And keep it still awake.

CHARLES: O may the least omission pain
My well instructed soul.

JOHN: And drive me to the blood again
Which makes the wounded whole.

(The organ sounds the note.
The CHOIR sing the hymn through.)

CHOIR: I want a principle within
Of jealous godly fear,
A sensibility of sin,
A pain to feel it near.

I want the first approach to feel,
Of pride or fond desire,
To catch the wandering of my soul
And quench the kindling fire.

That I from thee no more may part,
No more they goodness grieve,
The filial awe the fleshly heart
The tender conscience give.

Quick as the apple of an eye
Oh God my conscience make.

Awake my soul, when sin is nigh
And keep it still awake.

O may the least omission pain
My well instructed soul
And drive me to the blood again
Which makes the wounded whole.

(The CHOIR remain standing.)

JOHN: The English are too far gone in sin. Can I, being
myself confounded, bring them to God?

(A pause.)

I have decided! I will go to America and convert the
Indians!

(At once JOHN and CHARLES kneel in prayer.)

Lord! I will bring your word to the poor children of nature,
the savage Indians. Who live as we did in Eden, joyous but
not knowing.
My end in leaving my native country is not to gain the
dung or dross of riches or honour, but simply this – to
save my soul. To live wholly for the glory of God.

(The organ sounds the note.
CHOIR sing.)

CHOIR: And let our bodies part
To different climes repair.
Inseparably joined in heart
The friends of Jesus are.

The vineyard of their Lord
Before his labourers lies
And lo we see the vast reward
Which waits us in the skies.

(The CHOIR sit.)

SCENE SIX

During the hymn at the end of the previous scene, five actors
set up the boat. They form a boat shape, holding a rope
between them.
They play the SAILORS.
An announcement.

ANNOUNCER: LADIES AND GENTS. JOHN WESLEY SAILS
TO AMERICA TO CONVERT THE INDIANS.

FIRST SAILOR: Tell y'what, matey. Be a funny kind of cargo
this time out.

SECOND: What cargo's that?

FIRST: Cargo of a religious nature.

SECOND: What? Shipping Bibles out to the Indian?

FIRST: Bibles. And they to read 'em.

SECOND: Parsons?

FIRST: Parsons.

(JOHN speaks aside.)

JOHN: In the afternoon we found the good ship 'Simmonds' off
Gravesend, and at once went on board.

(JOHN and CHARLES go on board.)

THIRD: A load of parsons is a load of trouble.

FIRST: If the ship do sink, they'll come in handy.

FOURTH: I do hear we're taking on parsons.

FIFTH: Ar.

(Three MORAVIANS come on board.
They wear large black hats, black clothes.
They are a pastor, a boy and a woman with a baby in a
shawl.
Only the man speaks.)

FOURTH: And here come more of 'em.

FIFTH: Ar.

(The MORAVIANS and JOHN and CHARLES bow formally
to each other.)

THIRD: Hello, that's trouble.

SECOND: Trouble, why trouble?

THIRD: Not of the same sect, are they?

SECOND: What you on about?

THIRD: Their religion is different.

SECOND: All the one God, in't it?

THIRD: You dunno the half mate, not the half. Mark my words, we'll 'ave a religious war on our 'ands 'for we've kissed Land's End goodbye.

JOHN: Who are these fellows, Charlie?

CHARLES: Moravians. Simple brothers, Jack.

(JOHN bristles.)

JOHN: Simple?

CHARLES: Of a simple faith.

JOHN: They must be asses, to think Faith simple.

FIRST: Cast 'er off!

(JOHN in his way.)

Pardon me, sir.

JOHN: Simple? How simple? How can that be...

FIRST: Cast 'er off!

(JOHN is oblivious to the ship's workings.)

JOHN: Man has lived ten thousand years in sin. Ten thousand years, the Devil, he's been at it. We are ages deep in the Devil's work. He's wound the knot!

FIRST: Talking o' knots I got this boat 'ere, y'see. I got to untie 'er you see, sir, sail 'er 'cross the Atlantic. Which I can't be getting on with if she be tied up to Gravesend Pier.

(Pause.)

Sir.

(JOHN stares at him and stands aside.)

God 'elp us if we have a storm.

(CHARLES speaks aside.)

CHARLES: On Sunday, it being fair weather and calm, we did sail from England.

(The voyage begins.
Two effects: the sailors move with a motion of a ship; a blue cloth is rippled along the nearside of the 'ship'.)

JOHN: Our common way of living was this. From four in the morning till five, each of used private prayer.

(They kneel briefly, then stand.)

From five to seven, we read the Bible.

(JOHN and CHARLES mime Bible reading.
They close the Bibles.)

At seven we breakfasted. On water. At eight, public
prayers with the crew of the vessel.

(Crew put their hands together, mumble.)

FIRST: Amen.

SECOND: Amen.

THIRD: Amen.

FOURTH: Amen.

FIFTH: Amen.

JOHN: From nine to twelve I did read Greek, and learn
German. The while, my brother writ sermons.

(CHARLES mimes writing sermons.
Stops.
NB: the way to get the effect here is to go fast, treat the
mimes as farce playing, for a few seconds and speak the
details of the routine out hard and clearly.)

At twelve we met to give an account to one another of what
we had done since our last meeting. And what we would
do before our next. At one we dined, but denied ourselves
wine or any meats at all. From dinner to four we read
and preached to the crew.

(JOHN and CHARLES go round to each of the sailors and
say 'Repent' into his ear.
Each sailor says 'Sir' and touches his forehead.)

FOURTH: They be going on at us a lot.

FIFTH: Ar.

JOHN: At four, evening prayer. At five private prayer. At
six reading the Bible aloud to passengers. At seven, eight
and nine exhortation with any who would hear. At nine to
bed.

(Change.)

Where neither the roaring of the sea, nor the motion of the
ship, could take away the sleep God gave us. Thus did we,
day by day, work with rigour.

(The ship becomes becalmed, the effects cease. CHARLES
and JOHN turn,
the MORAVIANS turn,
they bow to each other.)

JOHN: Sir I have long observed, on our journey, the great
seriousness of your behaviour.

(The MORAVIAN bows.)

You clean the lavatories.

MORAVIAN: It is good for our proud hearts.

JOHN: You wipe up the vomit of sick passengers.

MORAVIAN: Our loving Saviour has done more for us.

JOHN: It is difficult to mortify the will.

(The MORAVIAN spreads his hands.)

MORAVIAN: It is simple.

JOHN: Sir! I would in all humility...

(The MORAVIAN bows.
JOHN bows.
Then JOHN, harshly.)

Dispute. Does not the Devil follow this ship, even now is he
not under the keel? And do we not need rigour, method,
discipline to shut him off?

(JOHN continues.)

And is that a simple matter?

(But the MORAVIAN interrupts.)

MORAVIAN: My brother! One question.

(A slight hesitation,
then JOHN bows.)

Do you know Jesus Christ?

(Pause.)

JOHN: He is the Saviour of the World...

MORAVIAN: True. But do you know He has saved you?

JOHN: I hope He has died to save me.

MORAVIAN: Do you know that? Do you know that?

(JOHN turns aside.)

JOHN: I said. I said. 'I do. '

(The effects of the voyage begin again.)

But I fear they were vain words.

(The effects begin to build up.)

I do not know Jesus!

SECOND: Don't like look o' the weather.

(The CHOIR stand.
The effects become still more pronounced.)

FIRST: We're in for it! Strike sail!

THIRD: Strike sail!

SECOND: Batten hatches!

FOURTH: Batten hatches!

JOHN: I am not saved! I am not!

FOURTH: Looks like a foul 'un. Really foul.

FIFTH: Ar!

(The organ sounds the note loudly.
CHOIR sing.)

CHOIR: Jesu lover of my soul
Let me to thy bosom fly
While the nearer waters roll
While the Tempest still is nigh
Hide me O my Saviour hide
Till the storm of life be past
Safe into the haven guide
O receive my soul at last.

(The CHOIR wait until the storm effects have stopped completely.
Then sit.
A pause.
The people on board stand slowly - they'd knelt when the storm started.)

JOHN: Were you not afraid?

MORAVIAN: I thank God, no.

JOHN: But were not your women and your children afraid?

MORAVIAN: No. Our women and children are not afraid to die.

(At once.)

FIRST: Land!

SCENE SEVEN

The boat actors pack up very quickly.
The colonial Americans, a FARMER and TWO YOUNG
WOMEN come forward on one side.
JOHN and CHARLES are at the centre.
The 'boat' leaves them: they don't leave it.

JOHN: At last, America! And here are brave colonists to greet us. Friends, I have come to convert the Indians.

FIRST WOMAN: Indians? He say Indians? I feel faint.

SECOND WOMAN: Indians?

(She screams.)

FARMER: Sir, what would you with them damn animals?

JOHN: Why, preach to them.

(The FARMER is flabbergasted.)

FARMER: Preach to 'em? Preach to Indians?

(The SECOND WOMAN screams.)

JOHN: I know they are poor creatures, at play in the fields of the Lord.

FARMER: Sir, you may as well preach to an Indian as preach to my horse.

(Here the ANNOUNCER comes forward in an Indian head-dress. He stands at the side, impassive, looking at the audience.
JOHN speaks angrily to the FARMER.)

JOHN: They are God's children, as you or I!

FARMER: Animals! Get in the farmer's way. Worse than foxes or damn rabbits, is the Indian!

FIRST WOMAN: They're wild. They eat children. And they're dirty. They don't wash! And, and, they carry off white girls!

(The SECOND WOMAN screams.)

FARMER: We got a goddam country here. Ripe. Vast lands.
And it's ours, all ours! The Indian, he's a rat in the barn.
Farmers have a way with rats, dammit! And you, parson,
don't you go worrying your head about no Indians. You do
the christening, and the marrying, and the burying –

(Indicates himself.)

Of US. And keep the women happy with your tittle-tattle.

(The TWO WOMEN simper.)

FIRST: We like a nice young parson.

(She curtsies.)

SECOND: Tell us about the fashionable places. Bath, the
pump room.

FIRST: And is Beau Brummel still the wag?

SECOND: Are the dresses bunched this year or not?

FIRST: And this year are the ladies wearing wigs?

SECOND: And Mr Wesley.

(Giggles.)

FIRST: Mr Wesley, you are not married. Yet.

(She giggles.
The other WOMAN giggles.
Announcement – the actor still in the head-dress.)

ANNOUNCER: JOHN WESLEY HAD A BAD TIME IN AMERICA.
HE HET UP HIS PARISHIONERS.

FARMER: Baptizing babes by ducking 'em right under?

FIRST: He says that's how the Lord was done, in Jordan.

FARMER: 'E's a monster! And a damned fanatic!

ANNOUNCER: HE STIRRED UP THE WOMEN.

FIRST: Sophy! Why you going about in white dresses?

SECOND: Mind your own business.

FIRST: Why you going to church at five in the morning? And
always with a hymn book? And casting down your eyes,

and speaking all demure about your sins?

SECOND: Mary.

(Slight pause.)

Do you like his ginger hair?

FIRST: Sophy!

(They giggle.)

And what about Mr Mellichamp? And Mr Williamson?

(The FIRST WOMAN indicates the FARMER.
The SECOND WOMAN shrugs, looks from JOHN to the
FARMER and back again.
Goes to JOHN.)

SECOND: John?

(She puts her hand on his arm.)

JOHN: Sophy, I...

(JOHN looks at CHARLES.
CHARLES shakes his head sternly.)

Miss Sophy. I am resolved, if I marry at all, not to do so
till I have been among the Indians.

(She snatches her hand away.
Stamps her foot.)

SECOND: Then I'll marry Mr Williamson.

(She goes at once to the FARMER.
In dumbshow:
she curtsies,
he bows,
he takes her arm.
He leads her to the altar.
They begin to dance, slowly in each other's arms.
This goes on during JOHN's speech.)

JOHN: Charlie, it's all gone wrong. I thought I would be in
a land, savage but pure. Under the sky. Without God's
Word, but near to God.

(He indicates the dancing couple.)

And what do I find? A little England.

(An announcement.)

ANNOUNCER: AND IT ALL GOES REALLY WRONG.
    SOPHY, MARRIED TO THE BOORISH WILLIAMSON,
    LEADS A GAY LIFE.
    JOHN WESLEY DISAPPROVES.

    (JOHN raises his hand sternly, the other hand on his lapel.)

    SOPHY TELLS HIM TO GET LOST.

    (SECOND WOMAN puts her tongue out at JOHN, and goes
    on dancing with the FARMER.
    JOHN turns away and goes round behind the communion
    rail, CHARLES at his elbow.)

    AND THEN JOHN WESLEY, OUT OF THE HIGHEST OF
    HIGHEST ANGLICAN PRINCIPLES, THOUGH THE OLD
    WIVES OF THE COLONY SAID OTHERWISE,
    REFUSES 'EM COMMUNION.

    (The couple dance to the communion rail, and kneel down.
    JOHN waves them away.)

FARMER: 'E did turn us from the Sacraments! I'll sue 'im!
    Defamation of character, I'll take 'im to court! Sue 'im
    for a thousand pounds!

ANNOUNCER: HE DOES.
    JOHN WESLEY LEAVES AMERICA IN A HURRY.

    (JOHN and CHARLES vault over the rail to the centre of
    the playing area.
    The boat forms around them AT ONCE and of course
    pointing in the opposite direction to that before.
    The ANNOUNCER leaves a short pause while this is being
    done, then continues.)

    JOHN WESLEY LEAVES AMERICA.
    HE'S NOT CONVERTED ONE INDIAN.
    NOT ONE INDIAN ON THE SHORE TO SING A HYMN AS
    JOHN WESLEY SAILS AWAY.
    JOHN WESLEY IS A FAILURE.
    JOHN WESLEY KNOWS IT.
    HE BEGINS TO TEAR HIMSELF APART.

    (The ANNOUNCER turns away, gets rid of the head-dress.
    The motion of the ship and the sea effect start, but only
    slightly.)

JOHN: I have thrown up my friends. Reputation. Ease.
    Country. I have put my life in hand, wandering into strange

lands. I have given my body to be devoured by the deep, parched up with heat, consumed by toil and weariness. But does all this make me acceptable to God? Does all I ever did or can know, say, give, do, or suffer, justify me in His sight? No! No!

CHARLES: Jack, why are you all shut up in here?

JOHN: You told me once, shut up!

(JOHN tries to laugh.)

CHARLES: I told you too - Rubbish! Rubbish! Utter cant!

(Becomes conciliatory.)

Jack, you could do nothing for the Indians. You could not even speak their language!

JOHN: My conscience cuts me.

CHARLES: For no reason.

JOHN: Slice! Slice! I did see a surgeon once.

(He makes a gesture like a knife.)

Slice a brain.

(Turns on CHARLES.)

You can do nothing for me!

(Then more kindly.)

Charlie. Let me alone eh? Pray a little, eh. For me?

(CHARLES lowers his head sadly, 'leaves the cabin'.)

This, then, have I learnt in the ends of the earth. That my whole heart is 'altogether corrupt and abominable'. That 'an evil tree' cannot 'bring forth good fruit'. That 'alienated as I am from the life of God' I am a child of wrath.

(The boat begins to pack up fast, leaving JOHN alone in the centre.)

Anyone there? You! You! Anyone there? Oy you! Anyone there?

(The boat have packed up.)

Anyone there?

SCENE EIGHT

JOHN at the centre.
TWO DEVILS come to either side of him.
The DEVILS are men, and in modern dress, black raincoats.
They speak in a chivvying manner.
They should slightly overlap their sentences, cutting in on
each other.
The CHOIR sing the hymn with the greatest force they can
muster.
The organ sounds the note very loudly.

FIRST DEVIL: Jack.

SECOND: Jack.

FIRST: Brand plucked from the burning, and all that.

SECOND: Stirring it up at Oxford, and all that.

FIRST: The Indians, and all that.

SECOND: And all that.

FIRST: What you doing, Jack?

SECOND: What's the game, eh?

JOHN :L . .

   (He falters.
   The organ sounds the note.
   The CHOIR sing.)

CHOIR: Christ the Lord is risen today,
                     Hallelujah!
   Sons of men and angels say,
                     Hallelujah!
   Raise your joys and triumphs high,
                     Hallelujah!
   Sing ye heavens thou earth reply
                     Hallelujah!

JOHN: Who are you?

FIRST DEVIL: He talking to you?

SECOND DEVIL: Talking to you.

FIRST DEVIL: Talking to himself.

SECOND DEVIL: Jack, you –

(Puts his finger to temple.)

Touched?

FIRST DEVIL: All this ranting and raving.

SECOND DEVIL: Tearing yourself apart.

FIRST DEVIL: It's not healthy.

SECOND DEVIL: Getting you nowhere.

FIRST DEVIL: Thrashing about! Fasting. Shouting at every Tom Dick an' Harry 'bout their sins.

SECOND DEVIL: You gone out of your mind?

(Pause.)

JOHN: Get thee...

(The DEVILS laugh,
softly and nastily.
JOHN falters with the famous phrase.)

behind me.

(The organ sounds the note.
The CHOIR sing.)

CHOIR: Love's redeeming work is done,
                    Hallelujah!
Fought the fight the battle won,
                    Hallelujah!
Vain the stone, the watch, the seal.
                    Hallelujah!
Christ hath burst the gates of Hell,
                    Hallelujah!

FIRST DEVIL: You're alone, Jack.

SECOND DEVIL: The others.

FIRST DEVIL: Ordinary men and women.

SECOND DEVIL: Ordinary people.

FIRST DEVIL: All of 'em Jack, all of 'em. They don't know what you're on about.

SECOND DEVIL: Didn't you know that?

FIRST DEVIL: You've got a congregation of one, minister.

(He nudges JOHN.)

SECOND DEVIL: You.

   (He nudges JOHN.)

FIRST DEVIL: You.

   (He nudges JOHN.)

   The DEVILS laugh.
   The organ sounds the note.
   The CHOIR sing.)

CHOIR: Lives again our glorious King.
                  Hallelujah!
  Where, O death, is now thy sting?
                  Hallelujah!
  Once he died, our souls to save.
                  Hallelujah!
  Where's thy victory, boasting grave?
                  Hallelujah!

FIRST DEVIL: Jack, I don't know how to say this to you.

SECOND DEVIL: It's tough on you.

FIRST DEVIL: It's tough on you, but we got to spill the beans.
   You see it's all...

SECOND DEVIL: It's all...

FIRST DEVIL: It's all...

   (Pause.)

   A great big con.

JOHN: No!

   (From here to the end of the passage JOHN denies them
   more strongly.
   The DEVILS – this is difficult for the actors – maintain
   exactly the same pace and pitch in their lines, no matter
   how loud the JOHN WESLEY actor becomes.)

SECOND DEVIL: You've been had.

JOHN: Oh Lord! I am buffeted, I am beaten about.

FIRST DEVIL: Heaven up.

SECOND DEVIL: The other down below.

FIRST DEVIL: 'S not on.

JOHN: Out of the deep have I called unto Thee O Lord.

FIRST DEVIL: Yer Heaven an' yer Hell.

SECOND DEVIL: Ain't so.

FIRST DEVIL: Just is not.

SECOND DEVIL: Yer on yer tod, me old China.

FIRST DEVIL: On yer tod an' nowhere.

SECOND DEVIL: Vanity of vanities, saith the preacher.

FIRST DEVIL: All things are full of weariness.

SECOND DEVIL: Man cannot utter it.

FIRST DEVIL: There is no new thing under the sun.

SECOND DEVIL: That's the picture.

(JOHN speaks the lines from the Psalm fast – all this
section, with the DEVILS, is _fast_.)

JOHN: I wait for the Lord, my soul doth wait
And in his Word do I hope,
My soul waiteth for the Lord
More than they that watch for the morning.

(The organ sounds the note.
The CHOIR sing.)

CHOIR: Soar we now where Christ hath led,
Hallelujah!
Following our exalted Head.
Hallelujah!
Made like Him, like Him we rise,
Hallelujah!
Ours the cross, the grave, the skies.
Hallelujah!

(An announcement.)

ANNOUNCER: WINTER OF 1738. JOHN WESLEY HAD HIS
DARK NIGHT OF THE SOUL.
AND A FEW DAYS AFTER EASTER GOT WHAT HE
WANTED.

(The ANNOUNCER takes a book from someone in the front
row.
Holds it up.)

HIS DIARY.

(The actor reads.)

IN THE EVENING I WENT VERY UNWILLINGLY TO A
SOCIETY IN ALDERSGATE STREET. ABOUT A QUARTER
BEFORE NINE, I FELT MY HEART STRANGELY
WARMED.
I DID TRUST IN CHRIST, CHRIST ALONE, FOR SAL-
VATION.
HE HAD TAKEN AWAY MY SINS, EVEN MINE, AND
SAVED ME FROM THE LAW OF SIN AND DEATH.

JOHN: I cried out! And they fled away!

(Spreads his arms violently.
The TWO DEVILS whirl away to the sides of the playing
area out of sight.
Announcement.)

ANNOUNCER: AFTER ALL THE SERMONS AND TEARING
APART –

(He slaps the book shut.)

SIMPLE AS THAT.

(Organ sounds the note.
CHOIR sing.
JOHN goes up into the pulpit during this verse.)

CHOIR: King of glory, Soul of bliss,
                    Hallelujah!
Everlasting life is this,
                    Hallelujah!
Thee to know, thy power to prove,
                    Hallelujah!
Thus to sing and thus to love,
                    Hallelujah!

JOHN: I am...

(Points upwards.)

By God's deliverance, despite my sin, in a state of Grace.
The difference between this, and my former state is:
THAT THEN I WAS CONQUERED.
NOW I AM ALWAYS CONQUEROR.

(The organ sounds the note.
The CHOIR sing.
In the first verse, the WESLEY actor leaves the pulpit,

the other actors file off.
He follows them.
They're left with the CHOIR, who at the end sing 'Amen'
and shuffle out.)

CHOIR: I the good fight have fought,
   O when shall I declare
   The victory by my Saviour got
   I long with Paul to share.

   O may I triumph so,
   When all my warfare's past,
   And dying find my latest foe
   Under my feet at last.

SCOTT OF THE ANTARCTIC
or What God Didn't See

<u>Scott of the Antarctic</u> was first performed on ice at
the 1971 Bradford Festival by the Bradford University
Drama Group.

Characters

ANNOUNCER	THE DEVIL
KING OF ENGLAND	SNODGRASS, the DEVIL's devil
QUEEN OF ENGLAND	NEIL ARMSTRONG
GOD	SIR FRANCIS DRAKE
JESUS	CAPTAIN COOK
SCOTT	SIR FRANCIS CHICHESTER
BOWERS	DR LIVINGSTONE
EVANS	ROLAND, an anti-Scott figure
OATES	
WILSON	

Directed by Chris Parr
Costumes designed by Jeff Nuttall and made by Mary
Restieaux
Tape by John Dowling
Lighting by Roland Miller
Music written and performed by the New Portable House Band

As the audience come in, from the band snatches of the
numbers they will play during the show.
On the tape, wind noise. Occasionally in the gale the football
chant 'England, England'.
Nothing on the ice.
Dead ice lighting.

<u>SCENE ONE</u>. Buckingham Palace

Song, of 'God in his Heaven' and 'All right with the World'.
Then in the background Royal music, perhaps 'Land of Hope

and Glory'. In this and other scenes the speech has to be heard above this background. It should be muted, distorted, an audible backcloth.

ANNOUNCER: Ladies and gentlemen, in Buckingham Palace at dead of night, the King of England goes sleepwalking.

(Follow spot on the KING. He is in a nightdress.)

KING: Nightmare!

QUEEN: George!

KING: The Royal Nightmare!

QUEEN: George the Fifth! And what are you doing?

KING: M'gunboats! M'gunboats!

(Follow spot on the QUEEN.)

QUEEN: George! Remember you're the King of England, and stop that at once and come back to bed. If the King cannot behave like a king, where will we be?

KING: M'gunboats guns, they've all gone limp.

QUEEN: Where will we be?

KING: Nightmare! M'soldiers all dead.

QUEEN: Running 'round Buckingham Palace in your nightie. What will the servants think?

KING: The Union Jack drips with blood!

QUEEN: Poor simple souls. Their king running about at three in the morning in his nightie. We owe it to the servants not to stretch their loyalty.

KING: Madam!

QUEEN: Yes George?

KING: Shut your regal cakehole, you royal old bag.

QUEEN: Oh!

(The KING wakes with a start.)

KING: What?

(The KING looks about, then down at his nightdress.)

Running 'round Buckingham Palace in me nightie? Gad, what will the servants think?

(Clutches his head.)

Flames! Peoples of the world, jabbering! Heads of the
Grenadier Guards stuck on sticks! Colonial administrators
boiling in big cooking pots!

(Cringing.)

Oh Mary, Mary, I had a bad dream.

(Demented again.)

Quick, look out the window, and tell me – is it still there?

QUEEN: Is what still there?

KING: The British Empire.

QUEEN: Of course the British Empire is still there.

KING: Go and look!

QUEEN: George the Fifth, you're going the same way as
George the Third. Right round the bend.

KING: Look, you silly old majestic moo cow.

(He points, violently.)

QUEEN: Oh dear, oh dear.

(She looks out of the window, that is she looks, hand to
brow, in several directions.)

KING: I dreamed the half of the world that's English went...

(Claps his hands. 'Bom' on a drum.)

Foreign!

(To the QUEEN.)

Is the British Empire still there?

QUEEN: How could it not be?

KING: I'm not a happy King. I'll go to Westminster Abbey.

QUEEN: At three o'clock in the morning?

K ING: Westminster Abbey! And I'll pray to God, that the
British Empire will last forever, bigger and bigger and
bigger.

(The KING rushes out of his spot.)

QUEEN: George the Third! They shaved off all that King's

royal hair. Put hot irons on the royal legs. Leather straps, in the royal mouth.

(The two spots black out.)

SCENE TWO. Westminster Abbey

Song. Like the nursery rhyme 'The King is in his Counting House', but of the King in his church.
After the song, background church music, the same backcloth effect as in Scene One.
Stained glass window lighting.
Follow spot on the KING, kneeling.

KING: Lord hear our intercession, Lord God, that this
    majesty will not pass from the earth, that people of all
    climes may kneel, forever C. of E., in Thy divine light
    beneath the British flag.

    (The KING's voice repeats that, as the church music swells.
    He repeats the prayer again, the music very loud.
    The band play a chorus of their 'God is in his Heaven' song.
    The din becomes intolerable, begins to feed back.
    It stops suddenly, at the same time the follow spot and
    the church lighting go out.
    Background heavenly music.)

SCENE THREE. Heaven

Spot on GOD.
He's an old man in a wheel chair, which is pushed by an angel.

GOD: Jesus!

    (The chair pushed about fast.)

    Jesus!

    (The chair pushed about fast.)

    JESUS!

    (Spot on JESUS. He is pulling a big cross, cheerfully.)

JESUS: Yes Dad?

    (He puts the cross down. Lies on it, legs crossed and

hands behind his head.)

GOD: I'm putting you down for Eton.

JESUS: Oh Dad, you're an Englishman.

(GOD suddenly Jewish.)

GOD: I've been many things in my time, my boy.

(Drops Jewishness.)

How are the hands, son?

JESUS: Itchy.

GOD: I'll never forgive myself.

JESUS: Don't worry. I've got my...

(Holds up a big tube of Valderma.)

JESUS: VALDERMA!

(At once the two actors shout aside.)

GOD: VALDERMA!

JESUS: VALDERMA!

(They spell it out.)

V...A...L...D...E...R...M...A.

GOD: V...A...L...D...E...R...M...A.

(A bell tings, a CHOIR sings.)

CHOIR: Valderma, for cuts and sores.

(A bell tings.)

GOD: Woops!

JESUS: What happened? What happened?

GOD: I had a prayer from the King of England. Westminster
Abbey shakes to his anguished cries.

JESUS: What's on the old geezer's mind?

GOD: The British Empire.

JESUS: And what's up with the British Empire?

GOD: It's not big enough.

JESUS: Jesus Christ. I mean Me Me. The British Empire
covers half the world.

(GOD depressed.)

GOD: I know, I know. Cop a load of this.

(From beneath his skirts GOD kicks a large globe of the world – a painted ball. JESUS picks it up.)

JESUS: Oh look! The world.

(JESUS blows on the world.)

Hurricane!

(JESUS bounces the world.)

Earthquake, tidal wave!

(JESUS pokes the world with his finger.)

Krakatoa East of Java!

(GOD clutches his head.)

GOD: Don't do that. The prayers of the dying give me a migraine.

(A bell tings, a CHOIR sings.)

CHOIR: Anadin, for headaches colds and 'flus.

(A bell tings.)

GOD: Look at the world. What do you see?

JESUS: Yuck, yuck, yuck! Some men eating steak, some men eating muck.

(GOD brushes that aside.)

GOD: Yuck, yuck, yuck! Give it a shake and look again.

JESUS: Right!

(JESUS gives the world a shake and looks again.)

GOD: What do you see?

JESUS: Soldier, soldier boy with the severed parts of his enemy. Click click the camera. Kid sucking a mum's cancered tit. And that man sucking stones and that woman getting born a bundle of bones. And unfair rents, and jungle cities, and agricultural land defoliated, and workers and poets in the gaols, and fat men in the west and thin men in the east, all going outta their minds. Oh, yuck, yuck, yuck!

(GOD tetchy.)

GOD: Yes, yes, yes, yuck, yuck, yuck! Give it a shake and look again.

JESUS: Right!

(JESUS gives the world a shake and looks again.)

GOD: You see it now?

JESUS: Oh! I see it now!

GOD: You see it now!

JESUS: The British Empire!

GOD: The British Empire!

JESUS: The British Empire!

GOD: Bright and beautiful!

JESUS: One hundred million souls!

GOD: All in the Church of England!

JESUS: Gunboats on Seven Seas!

GOD: Union Jacks on Five Continents! Jesus!

JESUS: Dad?

GOD: Nip down to Westminster Abbey and appear to the King of England in a vision.

JESUS: Right!

GOD: Show him the world!

JESUS: Right!

GOD: And how British it is!

JESUS: Right!

GOD: And put the old bugger's mind at rest.

JESUS: Right!

(Follow spots on GOD and JESUS out.)

SCENE FOUR. Westminster Abbey.

Westminster Abbey effects, background music. Spot on the KING praying but standing up. His lips move but no sound.

JESUS's spot goes on. The KING is startled.
JESUS stands with his hands at his side and the world at his feet.

KING: Who are you?

   (JESUS spreads and shows his bandaged hands.
   The KING kneels.
   JESUS kicks the world to the KING.
   The KING gathers the world like a goal keeper.
   The KING holds the world up.)

   Gunboats on Seven Seas! Union Jacks on Five Continents!
   Oh Lord of Hosts, I thank thee for thy bounty.

   (But he notices something on the globe. He scrutinizes it.)

   But what's this white bit?

   (He reads from the globe.)

   An... Tarc... Tic... A? South... Pole? No Union Jack. No
   flag at all.

   (The KING kicks the world back to JESUS who scrambles
   for it.
   The KING, like a kid, throws a fit.)

   I wanna Union Jack at the South Pole!
   I wanna Union Jack at the South Pole! Gimme a Union Jack
   at the South Pole! Gimme, gimme, gimme, gimme, gimme!

   (Spot on the KING goes out. Spot on JESUS stays on.)

SCENE FIVE. Heaven.

Change from church to heavenly music, in the background.
Spot on GOD.

GOD: And was the King of England chuffed or narked?

JESUS: Narked.

   (GOD roars.)

GOD: Narked?

JESUS: The old man wants the South Pole.

   (GOD deflated.)

GOD: Where?

   (JESUS points at the globe.)

JESUS: The nasty white bit at the bottom.

GOD: But that's the worst place I made on earth.

JESUS: The old man wants it.

GOD: Let me think. Um um. Let me think. Um um.

   (GOD wheeled up and down chin in hand.)

   Um um. Um um.

   (Stops.)

   What we need is an English hero!

   (Follow spots go out.)

SCENE SIX

At once a fanfare.
Dead ice lighting.

ANNOUNCER: Ladies and gentlemen, men make their own
   history but they do not make it just as they please. The
   traditions of the dead generations weigh like a nightmare
   on the brains of the living. Therefore our hero, dying at
   the end of the earth in a dead white land colder than any
   ice-cream or ice-lolly, where even puss in the boils on
   your frost bitten fingers is hard like little yellow stones,
   did not know why he was there, or why he died, colder
   than any ice-cream or ice-lolly.

   (The fanfare.)

   Ladies and gentlemen! We give you our hero, Scott of the
   Antarctic!

   (On the tape bells peel. Mass singing of 'For He's a Jolly
   Good Fellow'.
   The Polar Party drag their sledge onto the ice. They wear
   clumsy snow shoes, not skates. They often slip up. Great
   pain, great difficulty for them. They often have to catch
   their breath.
   The tape stops dead.

   There is a recording by Sir Adrian Boult of Vaughan

Williams's 'Sinfonia Antarctica', with these words
spoken by Sir John Gielgud.

SIR JOHN GIELGUD: I do not regret the journey; we took
risks; we knew we took them, things have come out
against us; therefore we have no cause for complaint.

(Skaters come on. They whizz by the struggling Polar
Party and flash about the ice with the greatest of ease.
They go off after their piece.
SCOTT struggles onto a central position on the ice, as
long as it takes.
The Polar Party have megaphones round their necks. They
raise them to speak.
(If unamplified megaphones won't give enough volume I
don't see why the electrical kind can't be used – tho'
the colour of the kind I've seen is not suitable.
Perhaps they could be ... covered?)
At times they shout to one side of the building then the
other, see the direction marked 'Change'.)

SCOTT: All in good heart. And going well.

(Change.)

I said, all in good heart. And going well.

BOWERS: Jolly good.

EVANS: Bang on.

OATES: Wizard.

WILSON: Top hole.

SCOTT: All keeping our peckers up.

(Change.)

All keeping our peckers up.

BOWERS: Harry gooders.

EVANS: Great fun.

OATES: Just the ticket.

WILSON: Ripping wheeze.

(The Polar Party, change.)

BOWERS: Harry gooders.

EVANS: Great fun.

OATES: Just the ticket.

WILSON: Ripping wheeze.

> (Suddenly they collapse, all over each other.
> The exclamations fast and desperate.)

BOWERS: Jolly good!

EVANS: Bang on!

OATES: Wizard!

WILSON: Top hole!

BOWERS: Harry gooders!

EVANS: Great fun!

OATES: Just the ticket!

WILSON: Ripping wheeze!

> (And as they sort themselves out, spots on GOD and
> JESUS come up.)

JESUS: It looks very tough.

GOD: Of course it's tough.

JESUS: Hard.

GOD: Of course it's hard! Be no point if it was soft. I think
I'll drop the temperature.

JESUS: Poor sods.

GOD: Nonsense! They like it!

JESUS: They like it?

GOD: Love it. They lap it up.

> (Spots on GOD and JESUS go out.)

SCOTT: I say, chaps, it's better being out here, than lounging
about at home.

> (Change.)

I said, I say, chaps, it's better to be out here, than lounging
about at home.

BOWERS: Bang on.

EVANS: Bang on.

OATES: Bang on.

WILSON: Bang on.

SCOTT: By God's help.

> (Change.)

> By God's help with such young bloods, in the heyday of their youth, the Pole will be for England. Hurrah.

> (Change.)

> The Pole for England!

> (The Party, raggedly.)

BOWERS: Hurrah.

EVANS: Hurrah.

OATES: Hurrah.

WILSON: Hurrah.

> (The Polar Party trudge on, with muttered jolly goods, bang ons etc.
> Lighting off the Polar Party.
> Spots on GOD and JESUS.
> Off, a motorbike revs up.)

JESUS: What's that?

GOD: What's what?

JESUS: Zooming up on the horizon. A great black cloud.

GOD: Oh no! Not him!

> (Thumps his wheelchair in rage.)

> Oh! Bugger!

> (Spots on GOD and JESUS go out.)

SCENE SEVEN

ANNOUNCER: Ladies and gentlemen. We give you the Devil!

> (A motorcycle driven by a Hell's Angel. The DEVIL riding pillion, waving, is driven around the edge of the ice.
> On the tape, The Rolling Stones' 'Sympathy for the Devil'.
> The DEVIL dismounts, the Hell's Angel (SNODGRASS)

takes the cycle off. Comes back with a mike.
The actor doing the DEVIL takes the gag routines as far as
possible, adding material if he judges fit. He does a
diabolical laugh into the mike.

DEVIL: Ha ha ha ha!
All hear that? I'll do it again.
Ha ha ha ha!
All together, a-one, two three.
Ha ha ha ha!
A diabolical laugh moves the bowels wonderfully. One more
time.
Ha ha ha ha!

(Drops that. Drumroll.)

Snodgrass!

SNODGRASS: Wotcher want, yer scaly git?

DEVIL: This is Snodgrass. He's what's known as a psychopath.
Rides his bike all over the pavement.

(Drumroll.)

I thank you. Say hello to the nice people Snodgrass.

(SNODGRASS leans over the mike. Grips it aggressively,
early 'Presley' style.)

SNODGRASS: Hello nice people, I hope you all get knotted.

(Any reaction, boos etc. SNODGRASS goes for the audience.
Gives them a 'V' sign.)

DEVIL: He's so well brought up.

(The DEVIL drops that. Drumroll. What I mean here is
the mannerism of panto villains, of beginning again and
again with great seriousness. Exploit it.)

Snodgrass! I'm not happy.

SNODGRASS: Whatsa matter Devil, someone doing somefing
good?

DEVIL: How right you are, my leather crotched friend.
Someone is doing something good.

(Sick noises.)

SNODGRASS: Urrrgh.

DEVIL: Urrrgh.

SNODGRASS: Urrrgh.

DEVIL: Urrrgh.

SNODGRASS: Someone doing somefing good. Gor, don't it turn you over.

DEVIL: It is sick-making. Snodgrass! If you can move in those trousers without the police intervening, follow me.

(Drum solo as they walk to the Polar Party.)

SCENE EIGHT

The Polar Party are not moving, though they are struggling onward. They don't see the DEVIL and SNODGRASS.

DEVIL: There you are Snodgrass. English heroes doing good.

(SNODGRASS, at a loss.)

SNODGRASS: 'Ere. They going somewhere?

DEVIL: To the South Pole!

SNODGRASS: They must be...

(Searches for the word.)

Thick. Skat. Right out of their public school nuts.

DEVIL: And why are they thick, skat and right out of their public school nuts?

SNODGRASS: Nothing there. Is there?

(Gesture.)

Down the South Pole. Jus'...

(Searches for the word.)

Snow? Can't even bring it back home.

(Gesture.)

Melt, wouldn't it?

DEVIL: They're not going there for snow!

SNODGRASS: What are they going there for, then?

DEVIL: Honour.

SNODGRASS: 'Ow much is that a pound?

DEVIL: You don't understand. This...

(Points at the Polar Party.)

Is a moral quest.

(Suddenly all the Polar Party fall over.
Pause.)

SNODGRASS: Yeh. Well.

(The Polar Party try to disentangle themselves.)

'Ere. I got an idea. Let me do 'em. With me chain. No...

(Thinks. Then.)

Let me run me bike over 'em. Stamp me tyre marks, all over their navels.

DEVIL: Down, you swastika'd buffoon.

SNODGRASS: Don't you want 'em done then?

DEVIL: Of course I want them done.

(DEVIL rubs his hands.)

Horribly!

(From here to the end of the scene the hisses should be going again.)

SNODGRASS: Let me get me bike in then!

DEVIL: No!

SNODGRASS: Me chain!

DEVIL: No!

SNODGRASS: Me patent five pound steel tipped as worn by the U.S. Army cycle boots!

(Uncertain.)

No?

DEVIL: No.

(DEVIL in great good humour, puts his arm round SNODGRASS. Grandly to all.)

Snodders. All you nice people. Rest assured, don't get panicky, just don't worry, your heroes will be done.

(Hisses.)

Horribly.

(Hisses.)

They'll do themselves!

SNODGRASS: Yeh! 'Ow about that!

(They chant into the mike.)

DEVIL: Do 'em...

SNODGRASS: Do 'em...

DEVIL: Do 'em...

SNODGRASS: Do 'em...

DEVIL: Do 'emselves.

(Drumroll.)

SNODGRASS: Devil, give us another diabolical laugh.

DEVIL: Oh very well. Just let me get the phlegm among me molars.

(Summons his powers.)

Ha ha ha ha!

(To the audience.)

One more time, a-one a-two a-three.
Ha ha ha ha!

(They go off taking the mike with them to a drumroll.)

SCENE NINE

Drumroll goes into song. Hero rock.

SCOTT: Light's going.
Tent-ho, I think.

EVANS: About bloody time too, if you ask me.

(Change.)

About bloody time too, if you ask me.

SCOTT: I say, chaps, how about 'nother half mile. Just for fun.

(Change.)

Just for fun, eh chaps?

BOWERS: Spiffing.

OATES: Jolly good.

WILSON: Ha ha.

EVANS: Stuff that for a lark.

(Change.)

I said stuff that for a lark.

OATES: Oh don't be a wet kneed cheese, Evans.

SCOTT: Come on Taff, join in the fun. You know what I always say when the going's hard.

(All in unison.)

ALL: First... One... To... Drop... Dead... Is... A... Sissy.

(OATES to the audience on one side. WILSON on the other. BOWERS doesn't do this.)

OATES and WILSON: It's... Topping... To... Have... A... Leader... With... A... Sense... Of... Humour. Ha... Ha... Ha...

(Second heroic rock song. EVANS spits.)

SCENE TEN

The song done. SCOTT at once.

SCOTT: Tent ho!

(Change.)

Tent ho, chaps!

(They shout the call out to the audience.)

BOWERS: Tent ho!

OATES: Tent ho!

WILSON: Tent ho!

(EVANS spits aside, BOWERS, OATES and WILSON go to unpack the tent.
But EVANS stares at where his spit landed.

Spits, looks where that one landed.
Continues with this.
SCOTT aside.)

SCOTT: What luck it is to hit on such wonderful chaps. We
are an excellently found party.

EVANS: Eh boyo, look at that. Your spit freezes before it hits
the ground.

SCOTT: I say Evans, tent ho.

(Change.)

EVANS: Your spit freezes before it hits the ground.

SCOTT: Tent ho, Evans!

(But EVANS ignores SCOTT, spits again, watches his spit
fly through the air then catches it in his glove before it
hits the ground.)

EVANS: Like a marble.

(Change.)

Gob, frozen solid.

(Change.)

Like a marble.

(The others stop and stare at EVANS. He offers the marble
to them each in turn.
They are embarrassed.)

OATES: Cut along, Taff.

BOWERS: Yes, cut along, Taff.

WILSON: Yes, cut along, Taff.

SCOTT: Better cut along now, Taff.

EVANS: Let's all gob our own marbles.

(Pause.)

Have a game, eh?

(Summons up spit. Spits massively.)

Eh got an alley there! Three-er at least!

(Drops the good humour.)

Why not have a game eh, eh?

(Pause.)

Do what we like out here can't we? Not like at school, not like the army.

(They stare horrified. Pause.)

No headmaster, no high-ranking general going to come over the horizon, rap our bottles, call us naughty boys. Do what we like.

(Aside.)

We're all on our tod!

(Change.)

We're all on our tod!

(Downcast. Pause.)

Sorry I spoke I'm sure.

SCOTT: Buck up Taff.

BOWERS: Buck up Taff.

OATES: Yes, buck up Taff.

WILSON: Come on Taffy, buck up.

(EVANS chucks the bit of ice away.)

EVANS: Let's get the bloody tent up.

(He joins the others getting the tent up.
SCOTT speaks aside.)

SCOTT: I have every confidence in Petty Officer Evans.

(Change.)

A very strong and muscled chap. Heart of a lion.

(Change. Uncertainly.)

Heart of a lion. I have known him for many years.

(Change.)

Every confidence.

(Light change. Suggest the SCOTT actor sees ROLAND here. SCOTT turns to get into the tent. Then with a gush of enthusiasm.)

Gosh! It's wonderful to be here with such wonderful chaps.

(SCOTT sees ROLAND's SCOTT. He stares pleadingly.)

Wonderful, wonderful, good men.

(He gets into the tent.
Third heroic rock song. The heroes dream.
ROLAND – the 'other' Scott – hanging round the tent at
night.)

SCENE ELEVEN

SCOTT pokes his head out of the tent.

SCOTT: Rise and shine.

(Pokes his megaphone the other way.)

Rise and shine.

(They come tumbling out of the tent with great difficulty.
EVANS stays in the tent.)

BOWERS: Jolly good.

OATES: Jolly good.

WILSON: Jolly good.

EVANS: My bloody sleeping bag's like iron.

SCOTT: Low night temperatures.

(Change.)

Low night temperatures.

BOWERS OATES WILSON: Low... Night... Temperatures...
Very... Very... Chilly...

(EVANS at once.)

EVANS: My vest's like a sheet of iron.

(Getting annoyed.)

There are icicles in my armpits!

(Giggles suddenly.)

Hope I didn't have a wet dream in the night.

(Change.)

Make a nice ice-cream for the wife, eh?

(At OATES.)

Eh Oates, make a nice ice-cream for the wife.

(OATES incensed.)

OATES: I don't think that's called for.

EVANS: Shut your face, porridge!

BOWERS: Steady.

WILSON: Yes, I say, steady there.

SCOTT: Steady, chaps.

(OATES stiffly. He's a right tit.)

OATES: Can I have a word with you, sir?

(Change.)

Word in your ear sir?

(Change.)

Creep up your backside sir?

SCOTT: Oh very well, Oates.

(At once they step aside.)

What can I do for you, Oates?

OATES: It's Evans, sir. He keeps on calling me porridge.

SCOTT: I don't get it.

OATES: Porridge.

SCOTT: ?

OATES: Porridge Oates.

SCOTT: Oh! Porridge Oates. Ha ha.

OATES: I don't think it's very funny, sir.

SCOTT: Sorry old man. When it's fifty degrees below a chap
gets hysterical. Even a leader of men like myself.

OATES: Dash it, I don't mind a bit of a leg pull. Bit of a rag.
But Evans sir.

(Pause.)

I say, this is damned embarrassing.

(Change.)

The chaps and I feel sir, we all do.

(Pause.)

Petty Officer Evans is going potty sir!

(EVANS at once, aside.)

EVANS: I know Oates is telling tales.

(Change.)

Thinks I'm going potty.

(Change.)

And I am. I'm going right off my head!

OATES: Potty!

(Pause.)

Sir.

SCOTT: That's a dash serious thing for a chap to say about a chap.

OATES: Dash embarrassing.

SCOTT: Dash serious.

OATES: It is a dash serious thing for a chap to say about a chap.

(OATES suddenly loses control.)

Evans is a cad! And a little rat! And a great big bully! And he's going potty! Sucks yahboo!

(OATES, jumping up and down.)

Sucks yahboo! Sucks yahboo!

SCOTT: I say, steady the buffs.

(OATES, at once to attention.)

OATES: Sorry sir. When it's fifty degrees below a chap gets a bit hysterical.

SCOTT: Hold on, Oates!

OATES: I'm holding on, sir!

SCOTT: Whatever you do, hold on!

OATES: I'll hold on, whatever I do, sir!

SCOTT: Be at the Pole anyday now. Just hold on.

OATES: Gad it's hard.

SCOTT: Think of the King.

OATES: I'll think of the King sir.

SCOTT: If that doesn't work, think of your mother.

(OATES blurts this out.)

OATES: Evans says he sees things...

(During OATES's outburst, SCOTT looks over the ice at ROLAND. The tape starts a distortion of the final movement of 'Sinfonia Antarctica', as backcloth.)

Things on the ice sir. Unenglish things. In the crystal clouds. Dead men.

(SCOTT shouts this nonsense down. But still stares at ROLAND, who holds things up to him perhaps, or calls out.)

SCOTT: Your mother, man!

(Change.)

Think of your mother!

OATES: Yes sir!

SCOTT: Warm and sweet and good. Think of her!

OATES: I am, sir!

(Pause. SCOTT still looking at ROLAND. Then he rounds on OATES.)

SCOTT: When a chap's having a sticky innings, and a chap's wicket is at stake, a chap's got to know what matters in the world.

OATES: Gosh, you are a leader of men, sir.

SCOTT: I know. But I don't think about it much.

OATES: If I say you're super, you won't think I'm sucking up, will you sir?

SCOTT: Chap's got to say what he feels.

OATES: Gosh.

(Hand out.)

May I shake you by the hand sir?

(SCOTT grasps OATES's hand.
At once OATES screams with pain and sinks to his knees.)

Ahhhhhhhhhhh, mother mother mother!

SCOTT: I say Oates, something wrong with your hand?

(SCOTT still holding it.
OATES still on his knees in agony.)

OATES: Hand sir? No sir.

SCOTT: If something's wrong with your hand...

OATES: Thought of my mother Sir! Pain went in a jiffy.

SCOTT: If your hand's CROCKED...

(OATES picks his fingers out of SCOTT's grasp. SCOTT
watches. Pause.)

Be a bit of a blow...

(At once, from the others.)

BOWERS: Tent ho!

EVANS: Tent ho!

WILSON: Tent ho!

(The tent's packed up. SCOTT still looks at OATES's hand.)

SCOTT: Oh. Carry on.

(Change.)

Carry on.

(Weakly.)

Then.

(They're in their harnesses. They help SCOTT into his.)

BOWERS: Jolly good.

EVANS: Jolly good.

OATES: Jolly good.

WILSON: Jolly good.

(Lights on them dim.)

SCENE TWELVE

Through this scene their 'jolly goods' are ragged and breathless.
under the loud recorded voices of GOD and JESUS. Song.
Finale of the heroic song cycle.
Backcloth tape continues.
Spots on GOD and JESUS. They are watching the Polar Party
through binoculars.

GOD: Oates has got a nasty hand.

    (Pause.)

    Evans has got a cut hand.

    Lots of pus. Dripping out of his glove.

    Well, that's life.

JESUS: They don't go very fast. They sure...

    (Pause.)

    They sure they know what they're doing?

GOD: They're heroes. Course they know what they're doing.

    (The Polar Party all fall down. Spots on GOD and JESUS
    go down, lights on the Polar Party come up.)

SCENE THIRTEEN. Documentary.

The backcloth tape getting louder.
SCOTT's shout can just be heard above it.

SCOTT: Abnormal conditions!

    (Change.)

    Abnormal conditions!

    (The tape gets loud.
    And then abruptly from the distorted music to the
    ANNOUNCER, on tape here.)

ANNOUNCER: January the Tenth. The plateau on which they
    travel begins to slope. They descend...

    (Volume of announcement down.)

Three degree depot 9,892 feet above sea-level, one and a half degree depot 9,392 feet above sea-level, one degree depot 9,184 feet above sea-level.

(SCOTT above that.)

SCOTT: Things are not right.

(Change.)

Things are not right.

(Volume of announcement up.)

ANNOUNCER: The decreasing altitude brings strange conditions. Crystals make the surface very bad...

(Volume of announcement down.)

Crystals falling through the air. Crystals crystals crystals. Crystals bearding the snow ridges, lying loose on the snow.

(SCOTT above that.)

SCOTT: Unaccountable.

(Change.)

Unaccountable.

(Volume of the announcement up.)

ANNOUNCER: Crystals make the surface very bad. Like sand. As if they pull the dead weight through sand.

(The Polar Party in unison, distort the words 'sand' and 'manhaul'.)

POLAR PARTY: Saaannd.

(Change.)

Saaannd. Maaannhaul.

(Change.)

Maaannhaul.

SCENE FOURTEEN. Boredom of the March.

The Polar Party continues at random with the sand/manhaul effect.
A tape runs as below, with SCOTT's voice. Into it a wind effect. ROLAND - at work here? On animals?

TAPE: Boredom of the march. To each man sleeping boots.
Sleeping socks. Extra pair of day socks. A shirt. Tobacco
and pipe. Notebook for diary and pencil. Extra Balaclava
helmet. Extra woollen mitts. Buttons, needles, darning
needles, thread and wool. Extra pair of finnesko. Big
safety pins with which to hang up our socks. And for the
journey, nine-foot sledge. Cooker. Primus filled with oil.
Tent. Sledging shovel. Reindeer sleeping bags. Eiderdown
sleeping bag linings. Alpine rope. Bosun's bag, with
repairing materials, bonsa outfit, with repairing tools.
Personal bags, of fifteen pounds spare clothing. Lamp
box with one lamp for burning blubber, one lamp for
burning spirit, one tent candle lamp, one blubber cooker,
one blowpipe. Medical and scientific box. Two ice-axes.
Five man-harnesses. Instrument box. Five pairs ski
and sticks. One pickaxe. And expendable stores. 'Antarctic' biscuit. Cases for 'Antarctic' biscuit. Pemmican.
Butter. Salt. Tea. Oil. Spare parts for primus, and
matches. Toilet paper. Candles. Packing. Spirit.

(At the end of this scene, they have come to a dead stop.
Silence.)

SCENE FIFTEEN. Animals.

SCOTT: I wouldn't ask a dog to go through this.

(Change.)

No, I wouldn't ask a dog to go through this.

(EVANS erupts.)

EVANS: We're animals. What about us?

(Change.)

We're animals aren't we?

BOWERS: Oh, belt up Taffy.

WILSON: Yes, belt up Taffy.

EVANS: Woof! Woof! Woof!

(OATES puts his megaphone close to EVANS's ear.)

OATES: We've had just about a bellyfull Taff.

(EVANS weakly.)

EVANS: Woof. Woof.

(He slumps down on his backside.)

Give a dog a bone eh? Give a dog a bone. Give a good dog...

(SCOTT interrupts vigorously, broadcasting his speech all over.)

SCOTT: Now I know many of you must have little doggies back home.

(Change.)

Always ready with a lick.

(Change.)

Friendly wag of a silly tail.

(Change.)

Nuzzle his muzzle in his master's palm.

(Fiercely to EVANS.)

They've got no souls, you see, Taff! Poor doggies. Not like us Taff. We've got souls, and that's why we're here.

EVANS: I don't know what the fuck you're on about.

SCOTT: I'm on about...

(Change.)

I'm on about...

(Can't do it. The others come to his rescue. SCOTT weeps.)

OATES: We know, sir.

BOWERS: We're with you, sir.

WILSON: All the way, sir.

OATES: Right on down the line, sir.

(SCOTT dries his eyes.)

SCOTT: You're such jolly good pals.

EVANS: For crying out loud.

(Change.)

Let's get on to the bloody Pole, stick our flag up its bloody arse.

SCENE SIXTEEN. At the Pole.

The Polar Party resume formation and trudge on.
At once after EVANS' line, the ANNOUNCER.

ANNOUNCER: Meanwhile, unknown to Scott and his party,
the great Norwegian explorer Amundsen, with many dogs
on a low diet, had reached the Pole, and left the flag of
Norway.

(The DEVIL tiptoes with a great big grin to the centre of
the ice. Plants the Norwegian flag and a letter, and tiptoes off thumbing his nose.)

Scott and his party struggle on toward the Pole and their
bitter disappointment. Weaker than they should be, feeling
the cold to an intensity they did not expect, their destruction has already begun.

(At once, first skater's solo sequence.
During it the party inch toward the Pole.
The solo over, the Party are staring at the flag, Hangdog
faces.
After a long time, OATES takes the letter and reads it.)

OATES: Dear Captain Scott. Bags the Pole. First come first
served. Ha ha, hard cheese, love, Amundsen.

(Pause.
Then change. More hysterically.)

Dear Captain Scott bags the Pole first come first served
ha ha hard cheese.

(Short silence.
They all begin to sob quietly.
Build it up.
One by one they lift the megaphones so that their wailing
rises to a pitch. It stops.
Then all loudly in unison.)

PARTY: Captain... Scott's... Famous... Words... Dear...
God... This... Is... An... Awful... Place.

SCENE SEVENTEEN

At once, they turn away from the flag.
SCOTT's voice on the tape.

TAPE: Dear Diary. The Norwegians have forestalled us and are first at the Pole. It is a terrible disappointment, and I am very sorry...

(The tape begins to distort with elements of Vaughan Williams's score, the music for the coming skating solo.)

Very sorry for my loyal companions. All daydreams must go. It will be a wearisome return. All daydreams must go. It will be a wearisome return. All daydreams must go. It will be a wearisome return. All daydreams must go.

(The music totally established, the second skater's solo sequence.)

SCENE EIGHTEEN

Toward the end of the skater's sequence the DEVIL comes on. Spot on him. He carries a rugby football.
SNODGRASS fixes the mike up for him.
Skater off.

DEVIL: Ladies and gents. We give you the Madness and Death of Petty Officer 'Taffy' Evans.

(The DEVIL boots the football high over the ice.
EVANS watches it sail over. The others don't look.
EVANS's voice on the tape.)

TAPE: I think...

(Pause.)

I think they're playing rugby football with my head.

(At once, third solo skating sequence.
The following material is blended into the music. EVANS's voice: get the first phrase into the music almost at once, to set the device up.)

TAPE: Scrum down, scrum down, get down Evans.... Penalty goal! There goes my reason boy, right between the uprights... Hurt! Hurt! Injury time! Injury time!... I've got stud marks on my brain... Taffy Evans always played hard... Jock strap, jock strap, skull cap... No side, no side, whistle up ref no side... Heel heel... Studmarks on my brain... I don't want to play anymore.

(Tape music ends. Skater goes off.
EVANS sits down. The Party stop.)

EVANS: Can we stop a mo'.

(They stop without comment. All hang their heads.)

I've got an idea. It won't take long. I'd like to plant some
leeks.

(Pause.)

In the snow.

(Tape starts. EVANS's voice.)

TAPE: Nice bit of veg... Give you a nice bit of veg my ma
would say...

EVANS: In eighty-five degrees of frost.

(Tape, panicky.)

TAPE: I'm not letting you down boys... Thinking of your
tummies... A nice bit of green...

(EVANS shouts.)

EVANS: Something...

(Change.)

Living!

(Change.)

Something...

(Change.)

Green!

(Tape piling the phrase up dying away.)

TAPE: Was my valley/was my valley/was my valley...

(As on the ice, EVANS kicks his snow shoes off.)

SCOTT: Don't be a bloody idiot...

(Change.)

Put your snow shoes on, and catch us up.

DEVIL: And! They went on for a coupla hours, and went back,
and there he was, dead!

(Drumroll.)

I thank you. And now...

SCENE NINETEEN

The tape sound building up.

DEVIL: And now we give to you, the famous death of Captain Oates.

(Drumroll.)

Wait for the famous phrase folks.

(The tent bulges.)

Is it coming now, is it?

(Tent bulges violently. Tape gathering momentum.)

Get your hankies out! Really moving bit. Tears, the lot. Brave Englishman giving his life for his friends. Even I, ladies and gents, have a salty trickle.

(Tent bulges more violently.)

Yes! Here comes the famous phrase... Now.

(Nothing.)

Oh. Snodders!

SNODGRASS: Hello.

DEVIL: Get the famous phrase song sheet out.

(Two lackeys come on with a banner. It reads 'I am just going outside and may be some time'.)

Maestro, please.

(Very bad ugly chord from the band.
SNODGRASS sings horribly walking along the banner.)

DEVIL and SNODGRASS: I... Am... Just... Going... Outside ... And... May... Be... Some... Time...

(OATES's head appears out of the tent with megaphone.)

DEVIL: Here it is! Here it is!

OATES: I am just going...

(Tape getting loud.
SCOTT's head and megaphone pokes out.
Interrupts.)

SCOTT: What?

OATES: I am just...

SCOTT: What?

OATES: I...

SCOTT: What?

OATES: I...

SCOTT: What?

OATES: I...

SCOTT: What?

(That continues until drowned by the blizzard effect on the
tape.
OATES steps outside the tent but immediately collapses.
Into the tape the football chant 'England England' is briefly
heard again.
Figures of great explorers appear and approach the tent,
Armstrong, Drake, Livingstone.
They converge and tear the tent apart, fall on the Polar
Party's bodies and eat them.
Spots on GOD and JESUS come up at a great distance
blessing the spectacle.
And on the tape the blizzard turns to gobbling noises.
Spots down on GOD and JESUS.
Vaughan Williams at his grandest intervenes. The skaters
perform their final chorus around the heap of heroes.
Smoke fills the rink until all stops.
End of show.)

Other Methuen Playscripts

Paul Ableman	TESTS
	BLUE COMEDY
Barry Bermange	NATHAN AND TABILETH
	and OLDENBERG
John Bowen	THE CORSICAN BROTHERS
Henry Chapman	YOU WON'T ALWAYS BE ON TOP
Peter Cheeseman (Ed.)	THE KNOTTY
David Cregan	THREE MEN FOR COLVERTON
	TRANSCENDING and THE DANCERS
	THE HOUSES BY THE GREEN
	MINIATURES
Rosalyn Drexler	THE INVESTIGATION and
	HOT BUTTERED ROLL
Simon Gray	THE IDIOT
Harrison, Melfi,	NEW SHORT PLAYS
Howard	
Duffy, Harrison,	NEW SHORT PLAYS: 2
Owens	
Barker, Grillo,	NEW SHORT PLAYS: 3
Haworth, Simmons	
Henry Livings	GOOD GRIEF!
	THE LITTLE MRS FOSTER SHOW
	HONOUR AND OFFER
	PONGO PLAYS 1-6
John McGrath	EVENTS WHILE GUARDING THE
	BOFORS GUN
David Mercer	THE GOVERNOR'S LADY
Georges Michel	THE SUNDAY WALK
Rodney Milgate	A REFINED LOOK AT EXISTENCE
Guillaume Oyono-	THREE SUITORS: ONE HUSBAND
Mbia	and UNTIL FURTHER NOTICE
Alan Plater	CLOSE THE COALHOUSE DOOR
David Selbourne	THE PLAY OF WILLIAM COOPER
	AND EDMUND DEW-NEVETT
	THE TWO-BACKED BEAST
	DORABELLA
Johnny Speight	IF THERE WEREN'T ANY BLACKS
	YOU'D HAVE TO INVENT THEM
Martin Sperr	TALES FROM LANDSHUT
Boris Vian	THE KNACKER'S ABC
Lanford Wilson	HOME FREE! and THE MADNESS
	OF LADY BRIGHT